AURA GARDEN GUIDES

Karlheinz Jacobi

Patios and Window Boxes

AURA BOOKS

Aura Garden Guides

Patios and Window Boxes

Karlheinz Jacobi

Original German language edition:
Gärten leicht und richtig
Balkon und Terrasse
© 1992 BLV Verlagsgesellschaft
mbH, München, Germany

This edition produced by:
Transedition Limited for
Aura Books, Bicester
and first published in 2002

English language edition
© 1995 Advanced Marketing (UK) Ltd.,
Bicester, England

English language translation by:
Andrew Shackleton for Translate-A-Book,
a division of Transedition Ltd.,
Oxford

Typesetting by:
Organ Graphic, Abingdon

10 9 8 7 6 5 4 3 2
Printed in Dubai

ISBN 1 901683 59 1

Photographic credits
Apel 29 right; Bénary 15 bottom, 17,
18 left, 19, 20 left, 28 left, 28/29, 31
left, 33 right; Bloemenbollencentrum
8, 9; Burda 12/13, 25 top, 34/35, 42,
79; Caspersen 5, 37;
Celaflor 69; CMA 16
left, 21 bottom,
51; Eigstler 14,
24 left; Felbinger
28, 76 right; Haug,
Ammerbuch 58, 59;
Flora-Bild

backcover left; Henseler 82/83, 83,
84, 85, 86; Jacobi 13, 22 left;
Jeddeloh 38/39; Layer 90; Niehoff 30
top, 60; Photos Horticultural 87,
frontcover; Redeleit 15 top, 24 right,
27 left, 32, 56, 65, 66/67, backcover
right; Reinhard 2/3, 6, 11, 16 right, 18
right, 20 right, 21 top, 26 left, 43
right, 44, 45, 46, 49, 50, 52/53, 57,
70, 76 left, 80, 88/89, 89; Ruckszio
10, 25 bottom, 26 right, 30 bottom,
31 right, 32/33, 33 left, 40/41, 47 left,
55, 62/63, 74, 91, 94; Sammer 7
centre right, 27 right, 54, 56/57, 64,
67, 71, 95; Seidl 13, 22/23, 36, 81;
Skogstad 93; Stein 7 top left and right,
43 left, 47 right, 48, 72/73, 73, 92/93;
Strobel, Pinneberg 41

A display for all seasons

Just like 'ordinary' gardens, patios, balconies and roof gardens are ruled by the seasons. In summer, not surprisingly, they tend to be dominated by magnificent summer blooms in narrow window boxes. Yet even here, bulbs set in autumn — such as crocus, tulip, narcissus, hyacinth, scilla and glory of the snow — provide an attractive floral display in early spring. In March or April you can also buy bulbs that already have buds or flowers to provide an immediate display quickly and easily.

The pansy also flowers in spring, and often throughout the winter as well. It's now available in many beautiful varieties, and in March you can team it with daisies (*Bellis*), forget-me-nots and a whole range of primulas. However, the prima ballerinas of the early spring are the flowering bulbs and pansies. On a balcony they may start to flower as early as February.

The main summer season starts around the end of May or the beginning of June with those old favourites, geraniums, fuchsias and petunias, heralding a wealth of summer annuals. There are so many genera, species and varieties that balconies and window boxes can be filled with different plants every year.

For those who enjoy the unusual, specialised plants can create a paradise of fragrances on the balcony, or wild flowers can be used to attract honeybees, bumblebees and butterflies. Autumn, too, has some lovely days to offer: low-growing chrysanthemums and Cape heaths, bought in full bloom, will survive until the first frost. There's another, very special, kind of enjoyment for balcony or patio gardeners who create a real miniature garden in containers, using dwarf conifers. Winter heathers planted here will bloom in October, and continue flowering until March.

Of course, all these suggestions apply equally to bowls, tubs and troughs. The larger the container, the greater the range of plants available to you — indeed, you have much the same choice as you would in a garden. As the year turns, spring will reveal the same plants in flower on the balcony and in the garden. In summer, too, a balcony garden can display the same range of annual flowers and climbing (or trailing) ornamental shrubs. Vegetables, herbs, strawberries, even apples and kiwi-fruit — all can be grown on the balcony, turning a party there into a harvest festival.

Until the first frosts arrive you can still enjoy the long-flowering annuals: dahlias, tuberous and *semperflorens* begonias, geraniums, fuchsias and marigolds. Many plants will bloom for months, as you'll see in the next few chapters. By making a careful choice of plants, and thinking about their needs and their habit, you can transform a balcony, a window box or any other container into a real garden on a small scale — a garden for all seasons, where there's always something to see and enjoy.

Blue-flowered heliotrope, planted between standard privets, produces a delightful fragrance.

CONTENTS

Starting the season — the first weeks of spring

The patio season begins in spring with hardy pansies, daisies, forget-me-nots and primroses. Anyone with a nose for fragrance will also plant golden-yellow wallflower, if they can get it. As a rule these spring flowers are available complete with buds, flowers and healthy roots, which makes planting out and growing on considerably easier.

Daisies, pansies and wallflowers.

Pansies
Viola wittrockiana hybrids

Few other plant species produce as many different shades of colour as the pansy. Flowers occur in all sizes from the small to the very large. There are single-coloured varieties in deep (or delicate) shades. There are unusual colour combinations. There are flowers with interesting markings or variegated side-petals — and all of them ensure an intriguing display.

Even late autumn isn't too early to plant pansies that will cheer up thinly populated boxes, tubs and troughs. Make sure there's as much soil as possible left on the roots. The roots should be planted deeply, or the plants will become unstable and topple over. Pansies need an 8-in (20-cm) space between them, and regular watering. Regular dead-heading extends the flowering period.

Daisies
Bellis perennis

Daisies will produce white, pink or red flowers for weeks, often until the middle of May. They have no special requirements, and their small size (just 5–6 in/12–15 cm) means they are well-matched with spring flowers or dwarf shrubs. You can now buy single meadow daisies, too. All daisies flower in sunny positions or in half-shade. It's best to cut off dead flowers so the plant will produce new shoots.

Wallflower
Cheiranthus cheirii

These wonderful, velvety, sweet-smelling single and double flowers appear from March to May in shades ranging from pale yellow to dark brown. Some varieties will even bear orange and scarlet blooms. For windows and balcony boxes it is a good idea to use the dwarf bush types such as 'Tom Thumb Mixed', which are less than 12 in (30 cm) tall. Wallflowers go well with single-coloured, late-flowering tulips, with pansies and with forget-me-nots. They need a sunny or half-shaded position, 10-in (25-cm) spacing all round and a soil that's rich in nutrients. Regular watering and dead-heading will help to extend the flowering period.

Forget-me-not
Myosotis alpestris

The blue flowers of the forget-me-not make excellent companions for yellow pansies: the

Wallflowers and pansies

Right *Primroses in a tub*

plants are similar in size and have similar needs. Flowering in April and May, they also go well with tulips, narcissus, crocuses and other flowering bulbs that are left in their containers. Forget-me-nots are available in several shades of blue, and range from 6 in (15 cm) to 10 in (15 cm) in height depending on variety. In spring, if you're planting large plants with flowers in containers, make sure the roots have plenty of soil on them and are planted sufficiently deeply. It's always a good idea to water them generously before and after planting.

Primroses, polyanthus
Primula, various species

Polyanthus and primroses are available very early and flower repeatedly in many brilliant

colours. They are among the loveliest of the spring flowers, and you should never be without them — especially as they seem impervious both to rain showers and to sub-zero temperatures. These plants, too, need plenty of water. After they have finished flowering you can move them into the garden.

Everything in one window box: scillas, hyacinths and grape hyacinths. Pansies make a good accompaniment.

should can be just visible above the surface. Bulbs in containers are planted closer together than bulbs in the garden, but take care not to obstruct or cover up delicate winter aconites, crocuses and other small flowers with large-leaved tulips. Finally water them in.

Overwintering

Method 1: Put boxes or bowls in a corner of your balcony or patio. Cover them with at least 3-4 in (8-10 cm) of bark mulch, and use sacking or thick plastic sheeting for additional protection in frosty weather.

Method 2: Use a wooden box, and insulate the inside with rigid foam to protect it from frost. Spread a 2-in (5-cm) layer of coarse compost or bark mulch on the bottom and stand the bulb containers inside. Cover them with a 4-in (10-cm) layer of compost or mulch, and close the lid. This is the most reliable way to overwinter your bulbs, and you can use the box every year. However, don't keep this kind of insulated container in a heated storeroom.

It's important to check the moisture level of the soil inside the boxes throughout the winter: bulbs left in dry soil

Flowering bulbs

If you want flowers as early as February or March, and a fine display by April, fill your window boxes (or any other containers you can find) with hyacinths, the so-called 'botanical tulips', narcissi, crocuses and other small bulbs. There are two ways of doing this. You can buy pot-grown (i.e. flowering) crocuses, hyacinths, narcissi and *Muscari* from nurseries and garden centres in spring. Alternatively, you can plant dry bulbs in your containers in autumn, the way you'd normally plant them in the garden. This, of course, is a lot more fun. Use new containers so you don't

disturb geraniums and other balcony plants — and (as in the garden) don't move them until the foliage has turned yellow, i.e. when the plants have completed their development.

Boxes for bulbs shouldn't be too small. Make sure they have drainage holes covered by a layer of gravel or potsherds at least 1 in (3 cm) deep, to avoid waterlogging. Plant the small bulbs (snowdrops, crocuses and others) first, about 2-3 in (5-8 cm) deep, and press them in firmly. Always plant in groups — at least three to five of each species and variety. Unlike bulbs in the garden, larger types should be not be planted too deep in the soil, and the tips won't grow. Around late February or early March you'll see the tips of the first shoots. When you do, unwrap the containers and put them where you wish.

Suitable species for balconies and window boxes

- *Anemone blanda*, various colours, height 4 in (10 cm), flowering period March/April;
- Glory of the snow (*Chionodoxa*), blue, 4-6 in (10-15 cm), March/April;
- Crocus, various colours, 4-5 in (10-12 cm), March;
- Winter aconite (*Eranthis*), yellow, 3-4 in (8-10 cm), February/March;
- Snowdrops, white, 6 in (15 cm), January-March;
- Bulb iris (*Iris danfordiae*), yellow, 4 in (10 cm), February/March;
- *Iris reticulata*, dark blue, 6-8 in (15-20 cm), February/March;
- Dwarf and wild narcissi, various varieties and species, yellow, 4-8 in (10-20 cm), February-May;
- Scilla, blue, 6 in (15 cm), March/April;
- 'Botanical' tulips such as *Tulipa fosteriana, T. greigii, T. kaufmanniana* in many varieties and colours, 6-8 in (15-20 cm), with various flowering periods in March and April depending on species and variety.

 Keep bulb flowers growing until they die down naturally (or take the bulbs out of their containers when the flowers have died), and plant the bulbs in a shallow trench to finish their growing cycle and ripen off.

A feast for the eyes: tulips of different varieties with narcissi (daffodils).

Summer blossoms for the main season

Geraniums

(*Pelargonium hortorum* hybrids, *Pelargonium peltatum* hybrids)

Even in narrow balcony and window boxes, geraniums can provide a miraculous display of flowers. This is true both of the upright varieties (which rapidly fill their containers) and of the trailing geraniums, with their long, flower-covered shoots, which can drape a cascade of blooms over the wall of your house.

The colour range of these classic balcony plants is immense. The upright type alone has hundreds of varieties. It usually has large, soft leaves and flowers in shades of red, pink and white. Petunias, mini-marguerites, deep blue helio-tropes and other vigorous summer flowers go well with upright geraniums (see the list below). There are many ways you can use the hanging and

Still the favourites: geraniums.

semi-hanging varieties, which offer a choice of red, pink, white, multicoloured, single or double flowers.

Geraniums are absolutely reliable. They prefer full sunshine, but will also tolerate sites that are sunlit only for a few hours each day. The plants develop best in fresh soil. Only an excess of water will disturb the robust geranium; otherwise you can keep it for years, as long as it's overwintered in suitable conditions or propagated from cuttings. However, it's always a good idea to buy a few additional plants, so you can enjoy the attractive new colours and forms. Some geranium enthusiasts aren't afraid to add standard forms to their collection, though these are in fact completely uncharacteristic of the plant.

The top ten combinations with geraniums

1   Upright, red, double-flowered geraniums surrounded by mini-marguerites (*Chrysanthemum paludosum*); pink busy lizzie and yellowish-orange marigolds in front.

2   Upright, red, single-flowered geraniums interspersed with mini-marguerites; blue lobelia, yellow marigolds and gently trailing creeping zinnia (*Sanvitalia procumbens*) in front.

Trailing geraniums make a magnificent floral cascade.

3 Upright, bi-coloured, pink and white geraniums, interspersed with yellow slipper flowers (*Calceolaria integrifolia*); red *Dianthus chinensis* and white annual alyssum (*Lobularia maritima*), slightly trailing, in front.

4 Upright, scarlet geraniums bordered by a slipper flower on each side; (mixed) pink dianthus, two blue *Ageratum* and two slightly trailing annual alyssum in front.

5 Upright, brilliant red geranium, bordered by a dark blue heliotrope (fragrant) on either side; bi-coloured (red/yellow) *Lantana* hybrids, golden-yellow marigolds and white annual alyssum in front.

6 Upright, crimson geraniums in the middle, among mini-marguerites, pale yellow marigolds and pendulous, dark-blue *Verbena* hybrids (with a white eye) and creeping zinnia.

7 Upright, vermilion geraniums with yellow *Gazania* hybrids 'Mini Star', two pale mauve busy lizzies and cornflower-blue lobelia at the sides.

8 Upright pink geraniums with mini-marguerites (*Chrysanthemum paludosum*), white with a yellow centre, at the sides, golden-yellow marigolds in the middle towards the front, and finally hanging purple *Verbena* hybrids with a white eye in front of that.

9 Upright scarlet-red geraniums mixed with white, mauve-tinged star of the Veldt (*Dimorphotheca pluvialis*); at the front, Ageratum and red and white Lantana; in front of that, trailing, brilliant-red alyssum completes the combination.

10 Upright, lilac-pink geraniums with red *Begonia semperflorens*, brown gazanias, lavender-coloured busy lizzies and cornflower-blue lobelias in front.

Fuchsias

Fuchsias are available in single- and double-flowered varieties, in species with flower clusters and a pendulous, cascading habit, and in heights (or lengths) from 8 in (20 cm) to 20 in (50 cm). Commercial varieties come in every conceivable colour combination of white, pink, red, pale mauve, blue, and even a dark blue which is so deep that it appears almost black. Fuchsias offer marvellous opportunities for the enthusiast and the collector.

Even so, your first priority should be the habit rather than the flower colour — rigidly upright varieties are best used in borders or large containers. True pendulous forms belong in hanging baskets or on a balcony. Fuchsias show their flowers best of all when trained as standards. The charm of a fuchsia in flower is seen at its best in the crowded head of a standard.

The flowering period of fuchsias varies according to the variety, but generally lasts from May until the first frost. Fuchsias like to feel the breeze that fanned their South American ancestors at the edges of the forests and in the ravines of the Andes. They like to look down into the valley from the slopes. This is why they feel so much at home in window and balcony boxes. However, it's a mistake to believe that they don't like the sun; in fact they like to be in the sun as long as the soil remains moist. Once they become

dry they'll lose their flowers (and some of their leaves), the shoots will become woody, and the plants will take a break from flowering for six to eight weeks. If they're well cared for, they can tolerate a fair degree of shade too. Most species, however, like the sun, and some are decidedly sun-hungry.

Fuchsias are planted from mid-May onwards, preferably no less than 10 in (25 cm) apart. When you're putting the plants out in

spring, bear in mind that young, vigorous plants with their first blooms just opening are likely to grow on much better and adapt more easily to their new habitat than those already in full flower. Fuchsias like a rich, humous soil, and appreciate weekly feeding as soon as they start to grow strongly.

Some varieties tend to produce seeds; this weakens them considerably, so it's best to remove dead flowers and berries

as soon as you notice them. Ideally, fuchsias should over-winter in a cool, light position where there's as much moisture in the air as possible. Since the leaves are shed in winter, you can also put them in a dark room. Young plants with leaves, on the other hand, need plenty of light and temperatures around 60°F (15°C).

If they're in a room that's kept cool during the winter, fuchsias can survive quite well as long as

Fuchsias can have single or double flowers, and a wide spectrum of colours ranging from the brilliant to the subdued.

they're in a bright position and the temperature doesn't rise above 55°F (12°C). They can also overwinter in a well-lit cellar, shed or garage at 50°F (10°C), or if it is dark at not more than 45°F (8°C) (this also applies to a reasonably well-insulated attic). Other suitable sites include a cold frame covered with plastic, or of course a conservatory or a greenhouse. Some fuchsia enthusiasts swear by soil trenches 30 in (80 cm) deep:

the plants are buried in dry leaves, newspaper or poly-styrene chips. The trench has to be lined with narrow-mesh wire to protect it from mice, and covered over with soil.

From January or February onwards it's time to prune back fuchsias that have overwintered in the light by about one-third. Any that have overwintered in the dark are pruned in the same way from April onwards. Bring the plants into a slightly warmer place and water them lightly so the buds begin to 'break' or grow before you cut them back. Then repot them in fresh soil. At this point they need as much light as possible.

An A–Z of summer flowers

You can choose from a multitude of summer-flowering plants; you aren't limited to geraniums and petunias. Most summer flowers are grown as annuals: they start flowering in April or May (or are sold with buds and flowers at that time), and finish flowering in autumn or after the first frost, depending on species and variety.

If you enjoy sowing seeds, you can raise a number of these beautiful plants at home (see page 72). It isn't quite correct to call them 'summer flowers' — some of them provide a colourful display well into the autumn. Marigolds and busy lizzies, for instance, are continuously in bloom. Others may flower for just a few weeks. For this reason the plant descriptions below give the flowering period in each case.

The perennials — including fuchsias, geraniums, slipper flowers, lantanas and tuberous begonias — can all give pleasure throughout a long flowering period. Afterwards you can overwinter them or propagate them from cuttings.

Among the annual summer flowers there are also climbers and some hanging plants with attractive blooms. These are dealt with in separate sections. All offer many possibilities for new and varied plant arrangements each year.

Annual flowers such as gazanias, mallows, marguerites and others bloom just as profusely here as in the garden.

green, depending on variety.

Flowering period: July to September.

Position: Sunny, sheltered from the wind.

Planting: Keep well spaced (12 in/30 cm).

Care: Keep well watered and feed regularly.

Propagation: From seed from the beginning of April in a propagator or frame at temperatures of 60-65°F (15-18°C).

Floss flower, ageratum
Ageratum houstonianum

Light-blue, purple or rose-pink blooms on round, dense, bushy plants. Very prolific flowering. Height 3-6 in (8-15 cm).

Flowering period: June to September. Flowering period can be extended by cutting off the dead flower heads.

Position: Likes full sun.

Planting: 6 in (15 cm) apart.

Care: Water regularly but never excessively. Remove dead flowers. Feed every three weeks from mid-August onwards.

Propagation: From seed from January to March in a propagator at 65-70°F (18-21°C).

Love-lies-bleeding, amaranthus
Amaranthus caudatus

Unusual summer flower growing to a height of 25-40 in (60-100 cm), with dark, carmine-red leaves and long, hanging, tassel-like flowers in red or

Above *Floss flower (Ageratum) in a terracotta planter*

Below *Love-lies-bleeding (Amaranthus)*

15

Gold coin plant
Asteriscus maritimus 'Gold Coin'

An endless succession of brilliant yellow, coin-shaped flowers appear on the gently trailing stems, which are about 12 in (30 cm) long. The flowers stay open in dull weather and even tolerate rain well.

Flowering period: May to October, without a break.

Position: Sunny.

Planting: In nutrient-rich soil; suitable for hanging containers and to accompany upright, blue-flowered plants such as lobelia, heliotrope and blue petunia.

Care: Remove dead flowers regularly. Feed every fourteen days from the onset of flowering until the beginning of September. Perennial, so can be over-wintered.

Propagation: From cuttings.

Fibrous-rooted begonia
Begonia semperflorens hybrids

Flowers tirelessly. Upright habit. Numerous varieties with red, pink or white flowers in many shades. Also varieties with bronze-green foliage. Height 7-10 in (18-25 cm).

Flowering period: From June until the first frost.

Position: Full sun, but half-shaded positions also possible.

Planting: 6-8 in (15-20 cm) apart.

Care: Water regularly, but be careful not to overwater. Feed every fourteen days. Cut off dead flower heads.

Propagation: From seed sown in a heated propagator at 68-77°F (20-25°C) — but can be difficult: best to buy plants.

The gold coin plant (Asteriscus 'Gold Coin') flowers non-stop.

The same is true of the 'ever-flowering' Begonia semperflorens.

Tuberous begonia
Begonia × tuberhybrida

Perennial tuberous plants. Upright and hanging varieties with magnificent white, pink or red flowers. Many strains with double, single, fringed, frilled and striped flowers. Low-growing varieties are up to 6 in (15 cm) high, taller-growing types up to 12 in (30 cm).

Flowering period: June to October.

Position: They like half-shaded positions and will still develop their dazzling display of full blooms even in a completely shaded position.

Planting: In rich organic compost with no lime.

Spacing: 8-12 in (20-30 cm) apart, depending on size.

Care: Water generously, but do not wet the leaves (risk of mildew) and guard against waterlogging. Feed every fourteen days. When they have finished flowering in the autumn, allow the tubers to dry in the box and then keep dry overwinter in a small crate of sawdust or bark mulch. From March onwards, set the tubers in small pots filled with growing compost and placed in a bright, warm position.

Propagation: From seed in a heated propagator, or on a window-sill indoors at temperatures around 68-72°F (20-22°C).

In sunshine or in shade, tuberous begonias produce magnificent blooms.

17

Browallia
Browallia hybrids

Low-growing (8 in/20 cm) annual, dense bushy habit. Flowers are blue ('Blue Troll', 'Sapphire') or white ('White Troll'), and reminiscent of wide-open campanulas.

Flowering period: June to September.

Position: Sunny, sheltered from the wind.

Planting: 8 in (20 cm) apart.

Care: Remove dead flowers, feed only at fourteen day intervals.

Propagation: From seed at the beginning of May either in a propagator or on a window-sill indoors.

Slipper flower
Calceolaria integrifolia

Perennial, can be overwintered. Upright habit. This shrubby, yellow-flowered plant, 8–16 in (20–40 cm) in height depending on variety, is totally undemanding. The brilliance of its flowers is particularly impressive.

Flowering period: From June to October. You can ensure a longer-lasting display of flowers by removing spent blooms.

Position: Sunny to half-shaded.

Planting: Plant out 8–10 in (20–25 cm) apart, deeply and firmly in the soil.

Care: Feed each week and give plenty of water.

Propagation: From cuttings in August.

Cockscomb and Prince of Wales' feathers
Celosia argentea 'Cristata' and *Celosia argentea* 'Plumosa'

Upright with yellow, red or white flowers. 8–14 in (20–35 cm) high, depending on variety.

Flowering period: July to September.

Position: Need full sun.

*Browallia (**left**) and an arrangement of slipper flowers, gazanias and tagetes (**right**).*

Planting: 8 in (20 cm) apart. Do not plant individually: always group several plants together.

Care: Feed every two weeks from the beginning of June to the end of August. Only then will the magnificent bushes of feathery plumes develop by September. Take care to water in dry weather, since these annuals can't tolerate dry conditions.

Propagation: From seed, from March onwards, in bowls or pots in a propagator, or on an indoor window-sill at temperatures around 65°F (18°C).

Marguerite

Leucanthemum maximum 'Snow Lady' F1 hybrids

The pure white blooms are just as lovely as garden marguerites. This variety only reaches a height of 8 in (20 cm). Since it's a hardy perennial, it can overwinter in planting containers or in the garden.

Flowering period: July to August.

Position: Sunny to half-shaded.

Planting: In nutrient-rich soil, 10 in (25 cm) apart.

Care: Water regularly and feed

Left *Cockscomb likes to be on its own.*

Above *The perennial marguerite 'Snow Lady' is pretty, and also robust and frost-hardy.*

at fourteen-day intervals until the beginning of August. Remove dead flowers. After it stops flowering, plant it out in the garden or in a different container, returning it to the window box in spring.

Propagation: From seed on an indoor window-sill or else in a propagator at 68–77°F (20–25°C). Easier to propagate by division.

Yellow mini-marguerite
Chrysanthemum multicaule
'Gold Plate'

Only 8 in (20 cm) tall; dense, bushy habit with small, golden-yellow flowers. Varieties with white flowers also available. Ideal in arrangements that aim for a natural look.

Flowering period: July to October. Flowers continuously if dead flower heads removed.

Position: Sunny.

Planting: 8-10 in (20-25 cm) apart.

Care: Keep moist but avoid overwatering. Feed every fourteen days.

Propagation: From seed from March onwards on an indoor window-sill or in a propagator; may also be sown directly into boxes and pots. Raise at around 60°F (15°C).

White mini-marguerite
Chrysanthemum paludosum

Anyone fond of marguerites should go for this 10–12-in (25–30-cm) tall dwarf form.

Flowering period: May to August; after being cut back, September to October.

Position: Sunny, but half-shaded is also possible.

Planting: Late May/early June, spaced 12 in (30 cm) apart. These marguerites go very well with blue-flowered lobelia or with *C. multicaule*, which is of similar habit (see above). You can produce a very attractive effect by placing them next to blazing-red geraniums.

Care: Cut back in mid-August (once you've removed any dead flowers), water generously and feed at fourteen-day intervals.

Propagation: From seed in March in a propagator, or on a window-sill indoors at temperatures around 60°F (15°C).

Chrysanthemum multicaule *is the yellow mini-marguerite, while* C. paludosum *is the white species. Both are outstanding window box plants.*

Right *Golden camomile or feverfew*
(Tanacetum parthenium)
Below *Coleus and fuchsias*

Golden camomile, feverfew
Tanacetum parthenium

This chrysanthemum species is only 10 in (25 cm) tall. It has a dense, bushy habit, producing small, solid, pompom-like flowers in great numbers. 'Golden Ball' has yellow blooms; 'Snowball' has white ones; 'Aurea' has golden foliage.

Flowering period: June to September.

Position: Sunny to half-shaded.

Planting: Avoid soil containing peat — better to plant in a mixture of compost and sand. A lime-lover.

Care: Water regularly, feed every fourteen days (until August). Remove dead flower heads.

Propagation: From seed from April onwards in frames, a propagator or on a window-sill at 55-60°F (12-15°C).

Coleus
Coleus blumei hybrids

Perennial foliage plant, also a popular pot plant. Upright habit, 12-20 in (30-50 cm) in height.

Flowering period: The foliage, not the flowers, will provide the interest here.

Position: Sunny.

Planting: The colourful leaves of the coleus provide a welcome change from the green foliage of other balcony plants both before and during flowering.

Care: Coleus is easy to maintain and can even tolerate an occasional window box drought. Feed at eight- to ten-day intervals until the end of August. You can overwinter it successfully in a bright position indoors, but young plants are better looking!

Propagation: From cuttings from March to October; or you can sow seeds in spring at temperatures around 65°F (18°C).

planters. Varieties such as 'Baby Doll Mixed' with single- or multi-coloured flowers and other F1 hybrids such as the low-growing 'Snowfire' are in bloom all summer long. Average height 8–12 in (20–30 cm). Flowers continuously.

Flowering period: June to October.

Position: Sunny.

Left *You can buy pots of low-growing dahlia varieties that are already in flower.*

Below *The star of the Veldt is exquisitely beautiful.*

Dahlias
Dahlia hybrids

Low-growing dahlia varieties can be recommended for planting on a balcony as they have a long flowering period and are very robust. They bloom until the first frost. The varieties that are suitable for containers grow to a height of only 12 in (30 cm).

Flowering period: From July until the frost. However, you can buy plants that are already in flower as early as May.

Position: Sunny to half-shaded.

Planting: Dahlias require a container all to themselves be-cause of their extensive root systems, so don't plant anything else with them. Keep them about 12–16 in (30–40 cm) apart.

Propagation: By division of the dry tubers, making sure each piece has a bud on top. Also from basal cuttings or sowing seed in spring.

Chinese pink
Dianthus chinensis

New varieties with lovely colours have made this robust and free-flowering group of pinks even more valuable for window boxes and balcony

Planting: 10 in (25 cm) spacing in nutrient-rich soil.

Care: Water regularly, feed every fourteen days from June onwards, otherwise no special requirements.

Propagation: From seed in March/April in a propagator or on a bright window-sill at temperatures of 50–68°F (10–20°C).

Star of the Veldt
Dimorphotheca aurantiaca

Annual which blooms for weeks, producing bushy plants 10-12 in (25-30 cm) high with

yellow, white, orange or apricot-coloured flowers. Particularly charming is *D. pluvialis*, which has large white blooms with a bluish-violet centre.

Flowering period: June to September.

Position: Sunny.

Planting: After mid-May in nutrient-rich soil.

Care: Water regularly but not too much. Can tolerate occasional dryness. Remove dead flowers.

The new varieties of Dianthus chinensis, *the Chinese pink, are low-growing and have a long flowering period.*

Propagation: From seed from March onwards on a window-sill indoors, or in a propagator at 55–60°F (12–15°C). Prick out young seedlings into small pots, or sow three to four seeds in peat pots.

Cape aster, kingfisher daisy
Felicia amelloides

Dainty perennial, about 12 in (30 cm) tall, sky-blue daisy-like flowers. Blooms continuously.
  Flowering period: May to November.
  Position: Sunny.
  Planting: 12 in (30 cm) spacing in a nutrient-rich soil.
  Care: Moderate watering and feeding (every three weeks). Remove dead flower heads. When growing on, cut back to an inch or so in late autumn and begin feeding in March, when the new shoots appear. In mild areas you can overwinter outdoors, covering the plants over with bark mulch or straw.
  Propagation: From cuttings.

Treasure flower, gazania
Gazania hybrids

Modern hybrid gazanias have large blooms in many different colours, and are among the most beautiful of all summer flowers. New, low-growing varieties like the 'Mini-Star' group are highly recommended: they're 8 in (20 cm) tall, with flowers ranging from white, yellow and orange to pink or deep brownish-red shades.
  Flowering period: June to October.
  Position: Sunny.
  Planting: In nutrient-rich soil, and with no less than 8 in (20 cm) between plants.
  Care: Keep moist but avoid overwatering; feed every four-teen days from June to September.
  Propagation: Gazanias raised from seed bloom better and longer than cuttings. Sow seed in a propagator or on a window-sill at temperatures around 65°F (18°C).

Heliotrope
Heliotropium arborescens

Annual flower. Upright habit, plants up to 20 in (50 cm) tall, with dark blue flowers giving off a wonderfully aromatic scent of vanilla.
  Flowering period: June to October.

Left *Standard form of* Felicia
Below *Gazanias, salvias and pinks*

Right *Heliotrope has a wonderful scent of vanilla.*
Below *New Guinea impatiens with variegated leaves*

Position: 8-10 in (20-25 cm) spacing. Can put up with any soil, but prefers light, sandy soil.

Care: No special requirements. Feed at no less than fourteen-day intervals and water regularly. Can be overwintered.

Propagation: From seed in a propagator or on a window-sill (above a radiator) at temperatures around 65°F (18°C). Pinch out the tips of the seedlings when they reach a height of 3-4 in (8-10 cm). May also be propagated from cuttings.

New Guinea busy lizzie
Impatiens hybrids

Large-flowered, taller 'relation' of the busy lizzie, with a very attractive range of flower colours and (in some cases) coloured leaves. The plants grow into round bushes which branch vigorously, so they need plenty of space. You can also plant them in large pots so they can stand alone.

Flowering period: June to October.

Position: Half-shade to shade.

Planting: In nutrient-rich soil. Use large containers.

Care: Regular watering, feeding every fourteen days. Remove dead flowers. May be overwintered indoors.

Propagation: From cuttings in late autumn in a small greenhouse, or on a window-sill indoors (at 65°F/18°C).

Left *Busy lizzie all in white*
Right *A butterfly visits lantana blooms.*

Busy lizzie
Impatiens walleriana

The busy lizzies include taller (10-12 in/25-30 cm) and low-growing or creeping forms (6-8 in/15-20 cm). Flowers range from white, pink, and orange to scarlet, and may also be bi-coloured. There is a huge selection of varieties in a host of beautiful shades.

Flowering period: June to October.

Position: Sunny or half-shaded, but these plants will also grow in shaded spots facing away from the sun, where other plants fail.

Planting: Spaced 8-12 in (20-30 cm) apart.

Care: Water and feed generously and regularly.

Propagation: From cuttings (instead of overwintering) in autumn, or from seed sown in a propagator or on a window-sill at temperatures of 65-72°F (18-22°C).

Lantana, yellow sage
Lantana camara hybrids

Perennial shrublet with beautiful blooms in brilliant pastel shades. Flower colours include white, yellow, orange, pink, red, blue and purple, and tend to undergo chameleon-like changes in the course of the flowering period. Lantana can also be obtained as a standard.

Flowering period: Early summer until the first frost.

Position: Sunny.

Planting: Lantana will flower for several months if the soil is enriched with a well-balanced fertiliser. Set the plants 8-12 in (20-30 cm) apart.

Care: Once they are properly rooted, feed lantanas every week. From the end of September onwards, watering and feeding should be reduced to prepare the plants for their winter dormancy.

Propagation: Difficult: better to buy the plants — although can be grown from seed or soft cuttings.

Lobelia
Lobelia erinus

Annual, prolific flowerer. Blooms are a delicate light-blue to dark-blue, but can also be white or carmine red, with or without an eye. Upright varieties reach a height of 3–10 in (8–25 cm). Trailing lobelias can produce shoots up to 12 in (30 cm) in length.

Flowering period: June to October. The flowering period can be extended by cutting back the plants.

Position: Sunny to half-shaded.

Planting: 4 in (10 cm) apart. Do not use soil which is too rich in nutrients. Feeding at monthly intervals is sufficient.

Care: After the first full bloom, cut back by one-third; the plants will then flower again.

Propagation: Sow seed in March in a propagator or greenhouse, at temperatures around 65°F (18°C).

Annual alyssum
Lobularia maritima

These dwarfs, just 2–3 in (6–8 cm) high, cover the soil for months with white (particularly lovely), pink, deep purple or dark carmine flowers. I recommend the pure white variety 'Snow Crystal'.

Flowering period: June to October.

Position: Sunny, half-shaded.

Planting: Sow in April straight into containers (e.g. at the foot of climbers such as cup-and-saucer plant and morning glory). If the seedlings are too crowded, thin out till they're 4 in (10 cm) apart.

Care: Likes the soil to be dryish rather than too wet, and does not require feeding. Cut back to half its size shortly before the plant has finished flowering. It will then bloom again.

Propagation: See planting.

Left *Lobelias and Swedish vine*
Right *Annual alyssum*

Above *Melampodium*
Right *A white tobacco plant behind pinks and sweet alyssum.*

Melampodium
Melampodium paludosum

Throughout the entire summer these 8-16-in (20–40-cm) tall bushes produce yellow flowers similar to marguerites. This plant is very natural-looking, with the new shoots growing over the spent flowers.
   Flowering period: From June to October.
   Position: Sunny.
   Planting: Not too close together: about 12 in (30 cm) apart, in nutrient-rich soil.
   Care: Water regularly and feed every fourteen days.
   Propagation: From seed in a propagator or on an indoor window-sill at temperatures of 60-65°F (16-18°C).

Tobacco plant
Nicotiana × sanderae

The tobacco plant has been recommended for plant containers since the arrival of low-growing varieties such as the 'Domino Mixed' F1 hybrids. These have yellow, pink, red or white flowers and an eventual height of just 10 in (25 cm).
   Flowering period: July to October.
   Position: Sunny, sheltered from the wind.
   Planting: Plant out in late May/early June, since tobacco is very susceptible to frost. It needs nutrient-rich soil.
   Care: Give plenty of water in dry weather. Feed at weekly intervals from June onwards. Remove dead flowers.
   Propagation: From seed: raise the young plants in a propagator or on a window-sill.

This is difficult, so you may prefer to buy plants from a nursery.

Petunias
Petunia hybrids

This annual balcony plant offers an enormous range of upright and trailing forms. Giant-

flowered and double varieties are also a talking point. The flowers of some forms have fringed or wavy edges, while others may be single; some are multicoloured and others one-coloured. The upright varieties include dwarf forms (8 in/20 cm) as well as taller ones (20 in/50 cm). The colours vary equally, ranging from white, pink, scarlet and copper-coloured to the deepest purple-blue and pale-blue.

Flowering period: From the beginning of May until the frost.

Position: Full sunshine is rewarded by an abundant display of blooms, but these plants also do well in a half-shaded spot.

Planting: Plant 8-10 in (20-25 cm) apart, depending on size and variety, but no closer on any account.

Care: Your most important task is constantly to remove dead flowers. Upright varieties may need supporting. Water

Petunias have more flowers than foliage.

regularly, but never keep too wet. Give weekly feeds from mid-June onwards. This ensures an even more generous crop of flowers and extends the life of the plant.

Propagation: From seed from mid-January until the beginning of March in a propagator at 65-68°F (18-20°C). Raising from seed is difficult, so it's better to buy plants from a nursery.

Annual phlox
Phlox drummondii

If you like perennial phlox, I'm sure you will also be pleased with the small, scented annual varieties. Look especially at those that are only 6 in (15 cm)

Suitable for a window box: these annual phlox varieties are just 8 in (20 cm) tall.

('Twinkling Star') or 8 in (20 cm) tall ('Beauty Mixed'); these offer a long flowering period and a wealth of different colours.

Flowering period: May to October.

Position: Sunny, sheltered from the rain if possible.

Planting: Set in nutrient-rich soil, 8 in (20 cm) apart.

Care: Water regularly, and feed every fourteen days. Remove dead flowers.

Propagation: From seed in March on a window-sill indoors, or in a propagator at 60-65°F (15-18°C).

29

Creeping zinnia
Sanvitalia procumbens

These plants are only 4-5 in (10-12 cm) high. Yellow flowers with a black centre that look like tiny sunflowers. The 'Mandarin Orange' variety has orange-coloured petals. Creeping zinnia goes well with mini-marguerites and in arrangements with a natural look. Flowers continuously.

Flowering period: June to October.

Position: Sunny.

Planting: From late May onwards in good fertile soil.

Left *Salvia with brilliant red blooms.*
Below *Creeping zinnia is also a good trailing plant.*

Salvia
Salvia splendens

Annual flower with magnificent, brilliant red blooms. Upright habit; 8-10 in (20-25 cm) tall, depending on species.

Flowering period: If the flower heads are cut off after the first bloom, the flowering period can extend from June onwards over the entire summer.

Position: Sunny to half-shaded, sheltered from the wind.

Planting: The soil should be well-drained and quite rich. Plant 8-12 in (20-30 cm) apart.

Care: Water with extreme care: salvia tends to shed its leaves if it becomes too wet.

Propagation: From seed sown in the greenhouse or on a window-sill (above a radiator).

Care: Ensure sufficient moisture. Feed from June onwards at two-week intervals. Remove dead flowers.

Propagation: From seed in a greenhouse or on an indoor window-sill at 60–65°F (15–18°C).

Butterfly flower
Schizanthus × wisetonensis hybrids

The 'poor man's orchid' produces a surprisingly large number of small, beautifully patterned flowers in beautiful shades. I can particularly recommend low-growing varieties such as the 8-in (20-cm) tall 'Star Parade' or the equally small 'Dwarf Bouquet Mixed'.

Flowering period: July to September.

Position: Sunny, sheltered from the wind.

Planting: From June onwards in nutrient-rich soil.

Care: Keep moist, but avoid overwatering. Feed at fourteen-day intervals from June onwards.

Propagation: From seed, from March onwards, at low temperatures in a greenhouse, or on an indoor window-sill where there's always plenty of light.

Cineraria
Senecio bicolor

Annual foliage plant with shiny white, felt-like leaves. Upright habit. 8–16 in (20–40 cm) tall, depending on variety.

Flowering period: The flowers are not of interest: the

Left *The butterfly flower (Scizanthus) ought to be used more often.*

Right *Cineraria (Senecio) emphasises the brilliance of adjacent flower colours.*

charm of the plant lies in its 'silver' leaves.

Position: Requires full sun.

Planting: 8 in (20 cm) apart. Goes well with red geraniums or dark-blue petunias and, in autumn, with pink and red pot ericas.

Care: Don't be too stingy with the water! Otherwise no special requirements.

Propagation: From seed in March/April in a propagator or frame at temperatures around 65°F (18°C).

Flowering period: June to October.

Position: They're very happy in full sunshine, but also feel at home in a half-shaded spot.

Planting: Space them 8 in (20 cm) apart. If possible, the soil should be well cultivated but not too rich.

Care: They'll need regular watering and weekly feeding.

Propagation: From seed sown in small pots in February, on an indoor window-sill, or in a propagator at temperatures of up to 60°F (15°C), or outdoors in April/May.

Left *Nasturtiums can be natural-looking and prolific.*
Below *Small-flowered and large double-flowered marigolds.*

African and French marigold
Tagetes

Annual summer flowers that are just as important for the balcony (and just as pretty) as geraniums. There are so many varieties that you could spend a lifetime trying out new ones: sulphur-yellow, golden yellow or orange-coloured flowers with smooth or ruffled edges. Varieties of intermediate height are 12–20 in (30–50 cm) tall, low-growing varieties are 6–12 in (15–30 cm) tall. Single or double blooms.

Flowering period: Late May until the onset of frost.

Position: Full sun.

Planting: 6–8 in (15–20 cm) apart, depending on variety. Rich soil and weekly feeding are desirable.

Care: Keep uniformly moist. Dead-head regularly.

Propagation: From seed in March/April in a frame or a propagator, or on a window-sill at 65°F (18°C).

Nasturtium
Tropaeolum

Annual summer flower with upright and trailing varieties. Flower colours: pale yellow, golden yellow, orange-red to the deepest dark red. Single and double-flowered forms.

Above *Verbena blooms twice if the dead flowers are cut off.*
Right *Zinnias*

Verbena
Verbena × hybrida

The colour range of this half-hardy perennial extends from white to red, blue and purple. Choose either from varieties with a dainty habit or from spreading types. Particularly recommended are the compact-growing 'Dwarf Compact Blaze' hybrids, whose shoots don't flop around.

Flowering period: July to October.

Position: Sunny.

Planting: Plant out at 8-10-in (20-25-cm) intervals, depending on size and variety.

Care: Water regularly but never too generously; even on very sunny days, give just a little water. Feed each week. If all the dead flowers are removed in good time, verbena will bloom for a second time.

Propagation: From seed — this is difficult, so you may do better buying nursery plants.

Zinnia
Zinnia angustifolia

The low-growing varieties are ideally suited to patios and balconies. Particularly good are the dwarf zinnia 'Thumbelina', which is only 6 in (15 cm) tall, and the 'Peter Pan' varieties, which reach 12 in (30 cm).

Flowering period: July to September.

Position: Full sun.

Planting: Water very generously until the plants are well established. Plant in rich, well-prepared soil. If you're planting out into a window box, space the plants at 8-12-in (20-30-cm) intervals, depending on variety.

Care: Remove dead flower heads. It's absolutely essential to feed them every fourteen days during the summer (i.e. from mid-June to the end of August).

Propagation: From seed in March on a window-sill indoors, or in a heated propagator at around 68°F (20°C).

33

Summer merges into autumn

Some of the long-lived summer-flowering plants such as lobelias, begonias and marigolds can produce a surprisingly good display of autumn blooms, which will only come to an end with the first frost. However, by this time there are bound to be some empty spaces in your display; and to fill them there's a large selection of mostly low-growing, bushy chrysanthemums ready and waiting in a range of beautiful colours.

Some varieties can even outshine the more common balcony plants and summer flowers when it comes to brilliance of colour and numbers of blooms. Their big advantage is that you can plant them out when they're already in full bloom. Chrysanthemums with large or small white, pink, red, yellow, orange or bronze-coloured single or double blooms are especially suited to autumn, when temperatures are lower and humidity is higher.

The Cape heath (*Erica gracilis*) also brings colour into the dark days of the departing year. Half-hardy ericas, with red, pink or white bell-flowers, can also be planted in full bloom. But whatever you do, don't forget to start by plunging the root ball deep into water until it's thoroughly wetted. It's best to plant ericas without their pot; leave a space about the width of your thumb below the rim of the container, and water them in thoroughly. The position doesn't matter: ericas will flower in both sun and shade.

Heather (*Calluna*) is another plant that's sold in flower or full of buds during late summer and early autumn. It's a low-growing shrublet with red, pinkish-mauve or purple clumps of blooms. The flowering period of the heather is followed by that of the winter or Alpine heather (*Erica carnea*). Some varieties come into flower at the end of October, producing a display of blooms that can survive the harshest winter. The greyish-white foliage of *Senecio bicolor* offers a very effective background of leaves for these autumn flowers. So do the pretty, variegated or green-leaved veronicas (*Hebe* species), whose red, white or bluish-purple flowers are very long-lasting.

If you're looking for something special, go for the frost-hardy evergreen *Pernettya*. It's a small shrub about 20 in (50 cm) tall with attractive, shiny leaves. It's very decorative, and its abundant crop of white, red or mauve berries adds variety to the balcony or patio in autumn.

Chrysanthemums provide splendid autumn colouring.

Colourful window-box arrangements

Suggestion 1: Three red-flowered Cape heaths (*Erica gracilis*) and three variegated hebes — height 10-14 in (25-35 cm).

Suggestion 2: Five red and white Cape heaths (*Erica gracilis*) mixed, height 10-14 in (25-35 cm).

Suggestion 3: Five chrysanthemums in a mixed arrangement with yellow, red, white and bronze-coloured blooms, height 10-16 in (25-40 cm).

Suggestion 4: Three orange-coloured chrysanthemums and four silver-grey cinerarias, height 10-16 in (25-40 cm).

Suggestion 5: Three *Pernettya* with white and mauve fruits, and three cinerarias between them, height 20 in (50 cm).

Suggestion 6: Two *Pernettya* with red fruits accompanied by three variegated hebes, height 20 in (50 cm).

It isn't a good idea to plant ericas with chrysanthemums, because ericas need unusually large amounts of water. Never allow the roots of a heather to dry out.

All-year-round plants

Broad-leaved shrubs

A balcony container, window-box or patio planter that's on display throughout the year becomes, effectively, a garden bed. Broad-leaved and coniferous shrubs provide a green (and flowering) backdrop for changing displays of seasonal flowering plants. In spring these are primulas and snowdrops, 'botanical' tulips and scillas; in summer, from June onwards, geraniums and lobelias, mini-marguerites and begonias. And finally in autumn, when the full bloom of summer has gone, ericas and chrysanthemums are in flower.

Besides looking attractive, and breaking up the monotony of traditional plant arrangements, this also creates a more natural effect. It'll also mean considerably less work and expense for you. You'll only need to renew the 'framework plants' every few years; in fact, with care they can often be kept for ten or even twenty years. And these year-round plants have another advantage: the containers will still look good even in winter, no matter what shrubs you've planted, broad-leaved or coniferous — although a mixture of both is undoubtedly best.

Some practical points

If you want year-round displays in your balcony boxes, window-boxes or other plant containers you'll need to bear a few points in mind. For instance, the containers must be large enough: window-boxes, for instance, should be at least 8 in (20 cm) wide and deep. Other planters, too, must be big enough to suit the particular plants you want. If you try using smaller containers, with a smaller volume of soil, the plants can easily may dry out, or be killed by winter frost. Plastic containers aren't suitable: they lack insulation against heat in summer and cold in winter. The best thing is to use boxes and tubs of pressure-impregnated wood, reconstituted stone, terracotta or earthenware.

As with seasonal plantings, all your containers must have drainage holes. These should be covered with a 2-in (5-cm) layer of potsherds or expanded clay granules before planting. Never forget this drainage layer. If you do, the container will become waterlogged when it rains (or if you overwater), and this will severely damage the roots of the plants. A blend of soil-less compost and sterilised loam is a reliable mix for filling the containers — or, if loam is not available, John Innes No 3 potting compost. A box 30–40

Cape heath, summer heather and Pernettya with white berries

in (80-100 cm) long can take
two dwarf shrubs, but no more;
you must leave space for the
succession of seasonal plantings. The best time to plant
them is in spring or late summer. Don't forget to leave
enough space for watering at
the top of the container: you'll
need about 1 in (2-3 cm).

Ivies with various leaf shapes and colours are available.

Hardy deciduous dwarf shrubs for all-year-round planting (a selection)

Barberry
Berberis buxifolia 'Nana'
20 in (50 cm); evergreen.

Dwarf barberry
Berberis thunbergii
'Atropurpurea Nana'
12 in (30 cm) tall; blood-red
leaves; deciduous.

Summer heather
Calluna vulgaris
In many varieties with pink, red
and white flowers; height 8-20
in (20-50 cm), depending on
variety; flowering period August
to September; evergreen.

Winter heather
Erica carnea
Several varieties with pink,
red and white blooms from
November to April; evergreen.

Creeping cotoneaster
Cotoneaster dammeri var.
radicans
Prostrate, drapes very effectively over the container rim;
flowers in June; evergreen.

Creeping spindle, euonymus
Euonymus fortunei
Horizontal habit with climbing
shoots; can tolerate shade as
well as sun; variety 'Silver
Queen' has white-variegated
leaves; evergreen.

Broom
Genista lydia
20 in (50 cm) tall; produces
prolific display of yellow
flowers in May/June; deciduous.

Ivy
Hedera
The leaves come in many
different shapes and colours;
evergreen.

Lavender
Lavandula angustifolia
24 in (60 cm), with pale to
dark-blue flowers from July to
September; delicate, aromatic
fragrance from leaves and
flowers; evergreen.

Dwarf roses
In several very attractive
varieties and colours; on sale
already in bloom from May to
July; deciduous (see also pages
40-41).

Evergreen dwarf conifers for containers and miniature alpine gardens

Balcony boxes and other plant containers don't have to stand empty in the winter; the bluish-green or golden-yellow foliage of dwarf conifers can bring colour and life to them. At other times of year too, these small garden plants can provide considerable pleasure — for example, when they are in company with winter and spring flowers such as snow-drops, crocuses, early tulips, daisies and forget-me-nots.

Of course, not all dwarf conifers stay obligingly small, despite being sold as dwarf varieties. However, in the confines of a balcony or patio container they won't reach the same height or width as they would in the garden. As well as remaining smaller, they also grow more slowly, and you can restrict their growth by regular pruning. Yews *(Taxus)* and junipers *(Juniperus)*, false cypresses and dwarf arborvitae can all be cut back without affecting their appearance. Pines arc the easiest of all to prune — just cut back the year's new shoots by half.

'True' miniatures need no attention from pruning shears, or at least very little. They're rather more expensive than the 'ordinary' dwarf conifers, but since they're very attractive and easy to care for, the extra outlay is well worthwhile. Among them is *Picea glauca* 'Conica Laurin', a conical spruce which stays really small, and a delight-fully pretty globular spruce, *P. glauca* 'Alberta Globe'.

The miniature pines include a dwarf form of the Bosnian pine, *Pinus heldreichii leucodermis* 'Schmidtii', *P. parviflora* 'Adcock's Dwarf' and also *P. parviflora* 'Negishi', with blue needles. The dwarf mountain pines, *P. mugo* 'Humpy' and 'Brevifolia' are also attractive miniatures.

Among the white pines there is a dwarf with the name *P. strobus* 'Minima', and even the eastern hemlock is represented by *Tsuga canadensis* 'Cole'. Equally, there is a globular

Japanese red cedar, *Cryptomeria japonica* 'Vilmoriniana', and also a balsam fir, *Abies balsamea* 'Piccolo'. The false

Yellow dwarf juniper (left), columnar spruce (centre) or Chinese dwarf juniper (right) will ensure your patio balcony is green, even in winter.

cypresses (*Chamaecyparis*) and the junipers (*Juniperus*) offer the largest choice of varieties and forms (see the list below).

As in the garden, the otherwise undemanding dwarf conifers do require a regular water supply, even in winter: conifers, unlike deciduous trees or shrubs, do not have a period of total dormancy. Conifers don't freeze to death; in most cases they're victims of drought! Apart from the yews, which don't like south-facing positions with the sun beating down, all conifers can tolerate sunny spots.

Miniature false cypresses
Chamaecyparis

C. lawsoniana 'Ellwood's Pillar'
Columnar cypress, bluish-green foliage.

C. lawsoniana 'Green Globe'
Green-leaved globular cypress.

C. lawsoniana 'Minima Aurea'
Globular cypress with yellow foliage.

C. lawsoniana 'Minima Glauca'
Globular cypress with bluish-green foliage.

C. obtusa 'Juniperoides'
Dwarf Hinoki cypress.

C. obtusa 'Nana Lutea'
Hinoki cypress, golden-yellow foliage.

Miniature junipers
Juniperus

J. chinensis 'Echiniformis'
Globular to squat habit.

J. chinensis 'Robusta Green'
Columnar habit.

J. × media 'Golden Sovereign'
With yellow foliage.

J. communis 'Compressa'
Columnar form.

J. communis 'Gold Cone'
Spreading habit, yellow foliage.

J. communis 'Green Carpet'
Creeping juniper, green foliage.

J. conferta 'Blue Pacific'
Spreading habit, bluish-green foliage.

Roses

Turning container-grown roses into tub plants

If you want roses to flourish in boxes or other planting containers, the prime requirement is to give them enough space for their roots. Their vigorous root growth is quite different from the fibrous roots of traditional pot plants like geraniums and fuchsias. If possible, dwarf roses shouldn't be grown with other plants such as geraniums, because they need such a lot of water. However, if you're growing standard roses in large containers, you can keep them low-growing and team them up with robust annual flowers such as alyssums (*Lobularia maritima*) and creeping zinnia (*Sanvitalia procumbens*). This should certainly create a more pleasing effect.

Roses grown in containers need good soil such as John Innes No 3 potting compost. Water them generously, especially after planting and until they are well established. After three weeks you should feed them with a special rose food every fourteen days (until the end of August). If they are regularly supplied with fertiliser, you can cut them back after flowering and they'll bloom a second time, just like most garden roses. In late autumn take them out of their boxes and plant them in the garden, or wrap the container in a plastic bag filled with coarse compost or bark

mulch to keep them through the winter. You can put them back in the planters (or unwrap them) in March/April.

Dwarf roses are a match for the loveliest bedding roses.

So-called container-grown roses are raised in rigid pots similar to plastic plant pots, and they're ideal for use in tubs and planters. Simply drop the plastic container into an outer pot made of earthenware, and pack it round with compost if necessary. Now stand your 'classic' tub plant in the sunniest spot you can find and keep it generously supplied with water. Until the late summer, you should also provide liquid feed. Container-grown roses are

available in a large number of attractive varieties.

Standard roses 35 in (90 cm) tall are particularly suitable for this purpose. You can buy them in a magnificent range of colours, and choose bush or bedding types in many varieties. For the smaller balcony or patio there are half-height roses (24 in/60 cm) or mini-standards (16 in/40 cm); these are dwarf pot roses and ground-cover roses grafted onto a stem.

Dwarf roses for pots, tubs and window boxes

■ 'Snowball', white, with a hint of colour, 4-12 in (10-30 cm);

Dwarf roses, seen here in an earthenware container, are perfect for the patio.

■ 'Baby Maskerade', multi-coloured, yellow/red, 8-16 in (20-40 cm), very bushy habit;
■ 'Finnstar', orange-coloured, 12-20 in (30-50 cm), very prolific flowerer;
■ 'Rugul', pure yellow, 8-16 in (20-40 cm), slightly scented;
■ 'Little Artist', blood-red with white, 8-12 in (20-30 cm), low-growing;
■ 'Morena', salmon pink, 8-16 in (20-40 cm), vigorous, broad bushy habit;
■ 'Red Det 80', brilliant scarlet, 8-16 in (20-40 cm), broad bushy habit, very compact;
■ 'Scarletta', orange and scarlet, 12-20 in (30-50 cm), prolific

flowering over a long period;
■ 'Teeny Weeny', pink with white, 8-16 in (20-40 cm), bushy habit, very prolific flowerer.

Two groups of dwarf roses are also suitable for planting in boxes, pots and bowls. Meillan-diana pot roses remain small, and flower freely; colours include golden yellow, pale yellow, white and various shades of pink and red. Minijet pot roses are even smaller, and have smaller blooms in red, pink, white and yellow. Some dwarf roses can even be kept briefly indoors. They will flower there once, but not for a second time.

41

Annual climbers

Among the annuals there are many climbers with pretty flowers and foliage that can be used to good effect on a trellis, on the sides of your balcony or on the wall of your house. These summer flowers are both decorative and functional. They provide a screen (more of an impenetrable 'green wall' in the case of the cup-and-saucer plant and hops), but above all they provide a delightful display of blooms. The majority of these plants can easily be grown from seed.

Catstails

Acalypha hispida

Pretty hanging plant with bright-red, furry, hanging blooms; requires a certain amount of warmth.

Flowering period: July to September.

Position: Bright, but not full sun; sheltered from the wind.

Planting: Treat roots with care when planting.

Care: Keep uniformly moist, mist daily from June through to September and feed every fourteen days. Water less in winter, and keep the room temperature not below 60°F/16°C. Older plants should be cut back in the spring.

Propagation: From cuttings in a propagator or on an indoor window-sill at 60–65°F (16–18°C).

*Hanging geraniums and yellow slipper flowers (*Calceolaria integrifolia*) make a colourful mixture.*

Left *Creeping snapdragon*
(Maurandia).
Right *Blue Swan River daisy*
(Brachycome).

Creeping snapdragon
Maurandia barclaiana

Dainty climber for trellises,
walls and railings.

Flowering period: July to
September.

Position: Sunny, sheltered
from the wind.

Planting: Spaced no less than
12-20 in (30-50 cm) apart, or
the shoots become entangled;
put stakes in the planters
straight away.

Care: Feed every fourteen
days from June to August. If the
plants are home-grown, prune
back shoots of 3-4 in (8-10 cm)
in length to stimulate side-
shooting.

Propagation: From seed in
March on a window-sill, or in a
propagator at 65-68°F
(18-20°C).

Elatior begonia 'Charisma'
Begonia × hyemalis Elatior
hybrid 'Charisma'

A group of varieties with a
compact, free-flowering habit.
The plants flower throughout
the summer, producing loosely
double blooms about 2 in (5-6
cm) across. The flower colour is
either red or coral-pink, depending on the variety.

Flowering period: June to
beginning of October.

Position: Sunny to half-
shaded.

Planting: In rich soil, not too
early; plant is sensitive to low
temperatures.

Care: Feed every fourteen
days from July to August; water
regularly. Take care not to
overwater, and on no account
wet the leaves (there is a risk of
mildew).

Propagation: From seed, but
rather difficult; only successful
in the greenhouse.

Swan River daisy
Brachycome multifida

Dainty, aster-like plant which
has bluish-purple flowers with a
yellow centre. It's particularly
suitable for hanging baskets.
The very similar *B. iberidifolia*
has bluish-purple flowers with a
black centre.

Flowering period: June to
October.

Position: Sunny, sheltered
from the wind.

Planting: Plant in nutrient-
rich soil, preferably in separate
groups: other plants choke it.

Care: Keep moderately moist;
leaves turn yellow if plants are
kept too wet or too dry. Feed at
intervals of fourteen days.
Remove dead flowers.

Propagation: *B. iberidifolia*
is very difficult to raise from
seed, so it's better to buy it
from a nursery. *B. multifida*
can be propagated from
cuttings.

The cup-and-saucer plant needs support for its twining tendrils.

Flowering period: Throughout the summer; at its loveliest from June to July. It will then stop flowering for a little while before coming into bloom again, but not so prolifically as at first.

Position: Sunny, preferably sheltered from the rain. Take down the hanging baskets and stand somewhere out of the rain if there is a prolonged rain.

Planting: In hanging containers on their own. Mix soils containing peat with bark compost, vermiculite or perlite: this will prevent waterlogging.

Care: Cut back any base shoots which grow upwards; don't water too much (test with your fingertips); give liquid feed once a week.

Propagation: From cuttings.

Cup-and-saucer plant (cathedral bells)
Cobaea scandens

This annual creeper has very attractive large flowers. At first they are whitish, turning pale purple or wine-red later.

Flowering period: July to October.

Position: Plant out in a spot that is sunny but always sheltered. Also do well in half-shaded positions.

Planting: Plant in fairly rich soil.

Italian bellflower
Campanula isophylla

Bellflower with blue or white blooms which flowers over and over again. Can also be used as an indoor plant. Perennial if overwintered. Another very pretty plant is the hardy perennial bellflower, *C. carpatica*, with blue or white blooms. It can be planted in the garden when it has finished flowering.

Flowering period: June to July.

Position: Bright to sunny, sheltered from the wind.

Planting: About 8 in (20 cm) apart in rich soil.

Care: Give plenty of water. Cut back after flowering. From September onwards watering is reduced as the resting period starts. Winter quarters should be bright and as cool as possible, not above 60°F (15°C).

Propagation: From cuttings obtained when pruning: these grow best in summer.

Centradenia
Centradenia inaequilateralis 'Cascade'

This beautiful hanging plant has trailing shoots 8-9 in (20-24 cm) long which are full of single blooms in deep pink.

Care: They require weekly feeding and copious amounts of water. These plants need to be looked after.

Propagation: From seed in a propagator, or on an indoor window-sill from the beginning of March onwards at 65°F (18°C). It's best to sow three to five seeds in each small pot.

Ornamental gourd
Cucurbita pepo var. *ovifera*

Ornamental gourds have three points in their favour. They have fast-growing, long (6-13-ft /2-4-m) shoots with large leaves that will cover a partition with greenery; they have large, attractive flowers that look particularly effective on climbing trellises; and they have fascinating, single-coloured or striped fruits of different shapes. These, however, are not edible.

Flowering period: July to September.

Position: Sunny to half-shaded.

Planting: Sow gourd seeds from May onwards. Plant in threes, directly into the tubs or boxes, and cover with about 0.5 in (10 mm) of soil.

Care: Give ornamental gourds liquid feed once a week from June to August, especially if the plants are confined to a container. Ensure generous and regular watering: these plants have large leaves, and need more watering than other patio plants.

Propagation: See planting.

Tyrolean hanging carnations
Dianthus caryophyllus

Perennial. Hanging shoots. Can be overwintered at 41-43°F (5-6°C).

Flowering period: From May until the autumn.

Position: Most varieties cannot tolerate fierce sunshine, so plant only on balconies or patios that face east, west or north.

Planting: Hanging carnations prefer a soil rich in nutrients and prefer to be about 10-12 in (25-30 cm) apart.

Care: Protection from sun and rain and regular watering (especially on hot days) will help them to flourish. Feed every fourteen days from June to August.

Propagation: From cuttings in September/October. Soil: a mixture of potting compost and plenty of sand.

Ornamental gourds produce fruits in different shapes.

Chilean glory flower
Eccremocarpus scaber

One of the loveliest climbers that can be raised from seed. In sunny and warm years it produces shoots up to 10 ft (3 m) long. Needs support for climbing.

Flowering period: July to September.

Position: Sunny, sheltered from the wind.

Planting: From mid-May onwards in loose, sandy soil.

Care: Water regularly but never too much. Does not like to be waterlogged. Feed every fourteen days from June to August.

Propagation: From seed at the beginning of March on a window-sill or in a small greenhouse at 65-68°F (18-20°C). The seedlings should be set in twos or threes in small pots.

Midsummer daisy
Erigeron karvinskianus

If you like hanging baskets to look as natural as possible, choose this dainty hanging plant. At first its daisy-like flowers are white with a yellow centre; later they turn a delicate pink.

Flowering period: June to September.

Position: Sunny.

Planting: As far as possible in hanging baskets and on their own. They are crowded out by other, more vigorous plants.

Care: Water regularly but not too much. Give a weak liquid feed every fourteen days. No need to remove dead heads.

Propagation: From seed on an indoor window-sill or in a propagator at temperatures of 65-68°F (18-20°C) — or by division.

Blue Mauritius
Evolvulus convolvuloides

Magnificent creeper with pretty blue flowers. These last just one day, but to compensate they are produced in great numbers each day on this plant's hanging shoots. Particularly suitable for hanging baskets.

Flowering period: June to October.

Position: Light, half-shaded, no blazing sunshine.

Planting: Plant, preferably on its own, in a hanging container, with no companion plants.

Care: Water regularly. These plants can also tolerate dry conditions. Feed each week with liquid plant food. Cut back shoots which have finished flowering. These soon shoot again and continue to flower.

Propagation: From cuttings obtained during pruning.

The Chilean glory flower is ideal for climbing up tall tub plants.

Ornamental hop
Humulus japonicus

The flowers of the hop are insignificant, but it grows very rapidly and soon forms an impenetrable green wall. The tendrils of the green-leaved species grow up to 13 ft (4 m) long. 'Variegatus', a more attractive variety, has shorter tendrils and pretty leaves with an irregular pattern of white and pale green spots. The hop retains its leaves until the first frost.

Flowering period: August. The catkin-shaped, yellow flower spikes are not particularly decorative.

Position: Sunny; the green-leaved species also grows in half-shade.

Planting: Set two or three seeds in small pots in March, put in a warm place (greenhouse, indoor window-sill), then transplant into large pots. Provide stakes or a trellis for climbing.

Care: Don't overfeed, otherwise the variegated variety will lose its colour. Water regularly and generously.

Propagation: See planting.

Morning glory
Convolvulus tricolor

The funnel-shaped flowers are sky-blue, brilliant purple, wine-red or white. The shoots quickly reach a height or length of 6–10 ft (2–3 m) and have to be tied to stakes or trellis-work.

Flowering period: Incessantly from the beginning of July until September.

Position: They grow and flower best on sunny balconies. In this position, curiously enough, the flowers stay open longer on dull days.

Left *Blue Mauritius*
Right *Morning glory* (Convolvulus tricolor)

Planting: Morning glory can easily be raised from seed; sow it in mid-March, in bowls or pots on a window-sill. The seeds germinate after only fourteen days; prick out the plants in small pots, then from late May onwards move them into the boxes. Take care to tie up the shoots straight away on stakes or trellis-work, or they'll soon be in a hopeless muddle.

Care: Morning glory needs weekly feeds from June to August. The main prerequisite for good growth is regular watering and the removal of dead flowers.

Propagation: see planting.

47

The pods of the scarlet runner are a familiar and popular vegetable.

flowers over a longer period.

Care: Water moderately, feed for the first time four weeks after sowing, then every fourteen days. Remove all spent blooms regularly.

Propagation: see planting.

Scarlet runner bean
Phaseolus coccineus

In catalogues the scarlet runner is listed with vegetables, and it is usually grown just for eating. However, there are many decorative forms. The white-flowered varieties include 'Desirée' (stringless), 'Mergoles' (stringless) and 'Weisse Riesen'. But the red-flowered 'Polestar' (stringless) and 'Prizewinner' are more suitable for a patio. They grow rapidly, with runners 13 ft (4 m) long that always twine to the left.

Flowering period: July to September.

Position: Sunny.

Planting: Best sown direct into their intended containers from mid-May onwards. Set two or three seeds at a time, 12 in (30 cm) apart. The soil should be rich in nutrients.

Care: After the seeds have germinated set up a support of some kind (wires, strings or poles) for the twining stems. Beans are undemanding plants that will even grow in a cool summer. Feed at weekly intervals from the onset of flowering.

Propagation: See planting.

Sweet pea

Lathyrus odoratus

You should always have some sweet peas, for the wonderful fragrance alone. They can also offer a magnificent range of colours from numerous varieties. The climbing types grow best on wire mesh. There are also low-growing varieties, such as the 'Knee-Hi Mixture' (25 in/ 60 cm) or 'Little Sweetheart' (8 in/20 cm), which need no support.

Flowering period: June to September.

Position: Sunny.

Planting: From the beginning to the end of April set seed directly in plant containers, two or three to each hole, 2 in (5 cm) deep and 8 in (20 cm) apart in moist soil. Cover seedlings with bark mulch if there's a risk of frost. Once the first tendrils appear, provide them with some twiggy sticks or plastic net. Successive sowings at fourteen-day intervals will give

Lotus flower
Lotus maculatus 'Golden Flash'

Unlike the red-flowered *L. berthelotti*, this variety blooms all through the summer, producing yellow to copper-coloured flowers on long, trailing shoots (up to 24 in/60 cm).
Flowering period: June to September.
Position: Bright, but not full sun.
Planting: From June onwards in nutrient-rich soil. If possible, no companion plants. Suitable for hanging baskets.
Care: Water regularly, avoid the roots becoming dry. Feed from June to August.
Propagation: From cuttings, preferably after flowering.

Swedish ivy
Plectranthus coleoides 'Marginatus'

Fast-growing relation of the familiar green-leaved and up-right Swedish ivy; suitable for hanging baskets. Perennial, can be overwintered, but it's better to raise new plants from cuttings.
Flowering period: Flowers are insignificant; the effect is provided by its pretty leaves.
Position: Sunny to half-shaded; in winter bright (warm or cool), can be treated like a pot plant.
Planting: Needs plenty of space around it because it grows very vigorously. Also suitable for hanging baskets.
Care: Keep uniformly moist and feed from May to August.

Cut back before the frost comes, transplant in spring.
Propagation: Easily propagated from cuttings which can be taken at any time of year.

Quamoclit
Mina lobata

This climber, also sold under the name *Quamoclit lobata*, has pretty flowers and a long flowering period. Its vigorous habit (with shoots up to 16 ft/ 5 m long) makes it very suitable for trellises and railings.
Flowering period: July to September.
Position: Sunny, warm.
Planting: At the end of May, spaced 12 in (30 cm) apart.

Place directly beside its support, since these vines begin to climb immediately.
Care: Water generously and feed once a week from June to September.
Propagation: From seed from March to May on an indoor window-sill or in a propagator at 65°F (18°C). Sow two or three seeds in each small pot.

*Quamoclit (*Mina lobata*) is unusual and easy to train.*

Purple bell vine
Rhodochiton atrosanguineus

Annual climber; with support in a good summer it will form dense 'walls' full of flowers. Also suitable as a hanging plant. Support required for climbing.
   Flowering period: July to September.
   Position: Sunny, warm and sheltered from the wind.
   Planting: From mid-May onwards in nutrient-rich soil.
   Care: Water generously in summer, but avoid overwatering. Feed every fourteen days from June to September.
   Propagation: From seed in March on a window-sill or else in a propagator at 60–68°F (15–20°C). Place young plants in threes in pots or hanging baskets.

Scaevola
Scaevola aemula 'Blue Fan'

The rainproof flowers of this splendid hanging plant are purplish-blue and fan-shaped, on shoots 24 in (60 cm) long. The flowers retain their delightful blue colour for a long time. Perennial, can be overwintered.
   Flowering period: June to October. Some pruning can be done even during the summer, since new flower shoots are formed within a few days.
   Position: Sunny.
   Propagation: From seed on an indoor window-sill or in a small greenhouse at temperatures around 65°F (18°C). More readily available as plants.

Thymophyllum
Thymophylla tenuiloba

This makes a good flowering companion for the blue, daisy-like *Brachycome*; its leaves are just as dainty and it flowers for an equally long time.
   Flowering period: June to September.
   Position: Sunny.
   Planting: In nutrient-rich soil. Plant only slow-growing companions. Also suitable as a hanging plant.
   Care: Keep moderately moist; some leaves will turn yellow if the plants are too wet or too dry. Feed every fourteen days from June to August. Remove dead flowers.
   Propagation: From seed from February to in a propagator or on a window-sill indoors at 65–68°F (18–20°C).

Thymophylla tenuiloba *flowers profusely*

Solanum, winter cherry
Solanum muricatum

Member of the nightshade family. Unlike the lovely, blue-flowered species (see tub plants on page 76), this one is remarkable not for its flowers, but for its fruits, which are golden-orange with purple longitudinal stripes. These are edible and taste like melon. The shoots grow up to 18 in (45 cm) long.

Flowering period: The purple flowers appear from April onwards, the ripe fruits in August.

Position: Sunny to half-shaded.

Planting: From June onwards in spacious hanging baskets or wide (and deep) window-boxes. Needs plenty of space all around and a rich soil.

Care: When the plants begin to flower, start weekly feeds. Plenty of water required. Cut back after fruits have been picked.

Propagation: From seed or from cuttings, but it's easiest to buy young plants.

Black-eyed Susan
Thunbergia alata

This pretty annual climber with an eventual height of about 5 ft (1.5 m) has charming yellow, orange or white flowers. The shoots climb very attractively up frames, stakes or railings.

Flowering period: June to October.

Position: Particularly prolific flowering is achieved on a sunny patio.

Planting: Thunbergias need plenty of space, so plant them 16 in (40 cm) apart. As soon as they're planted give them a stake to climb on.

Care: Water regularly and always tie up carefully.

Propagation: Sow seeds in pot in March at about 60°F (15°C). Plant out in late May.

The shoots of the black-eyed Susan (Thunbergia alata) must be tied up regularly.

51

Climbing shrubs

If screening is important and you have the necessary space, it's possible to create a 'green wall' on your balcony or patio by using climbing shrubs. To do it you'll need fairly large containers: the best are round or rectangular troughs made of terracotta, reconstituted stone or wood, because shrubs develop far larger root systems than summer flowers. The soil needs to provide a constant supply of nutrients, so you should add slow-release fertilisers. (For more about shrubs and their care, see page 37).

Not all climbers can cling to a wall or climbing support without assistance. Only one or two of the Virginia creepers can manage it without help — for instance, *Parthenocissus quinquefolia* 'Engelmannii' and *P. tricuspidata* 'Veitchii', which can even get a hold on a smooth, vertical wall. Ivy is another plant that has no problems in this respect: the shoots produce aerial roots that grip the surface. Ivy, unlike all other climbers, is evergreen, so will give all-year-round privacy on a balcony or patio.

If you're fond of beautiful flowers, plant clematis. They are available in magnificent large- or small-flowered varieties (e.g. *Clematis montana* 'Rubens'). Remember to plant deeply and at an angle, so that the graft point is well below the surface of the soil. You should also keep the area around its base moist and cool at all times by covering the soil with a mulch of stones or even a paving slab. Dwarf shrubs and summer flowers can also provide shade, creating the same effect. Two more points: never plant clematis on the

Virginia creeper and climbing roses are here used to disguise and beautify a house wall.

south-facing side of the house, and never plant it closer than 12 in (30 cm) to a wall.

Fallopia baldschuanica is a particularly rapid climber, and produces masses of frothy white blooms in August. In the course of a single summer its new shoots can achieve a length of up to 16 ft (5 m) if growing conditions are good. You can let the flowering shoots cascade down from a balcony, or train them up high walls or supports. Despite an astonishing rate of growth, the plant needs little attention and is easy to please. However, you'll have to cut it back with increasing severity every year to prevent it becoming too entangled and taking over the garden.

Climbing roses are also valuable patio plants. They need supports that will allow you to tie up the shoots, which can be several feet long. Possibilities include trellises, pergolas or plastic-coated wires attached to the wall, to posts or to metal poles. Tie the shoots of your rose horizontally or in a fan shape. Climbing roses need a good supply of nutrients, since they have a strong root system and develop several new stems each year. The most highly recommended varieties are 'Laura Ford' (a mini-climber with fragrant golden-yellow blooms), the slow-growing 'Compassion' (salmon-pink), 'Golden Showers' (yellow), 'Ilse Krohn Superior' (pure white) and 'Sympathie' (scarlet).

Wisteria (*Wisteria sinensis*) makes a feast for the eyes. The fragrant, bluish-purple, hanging flower racemes adorn this high-growing shrub for weeks. Start by training the shoots up onto a

One of the prettiest wild species of clematis — a form of Clematis macropetala.

framework, then tie them in horizontally. Wisterias like full sunshine and rich soil. You must never let them fall victim to drought: so-called 'frost damage' is mostly due to lack of water. It's important to prune wisteria regularly, cutting the new shoots back to about 6 or 8 leaves in late July. In winter you should thin out older plants, and cut back the stems already pruned in summer to just two buds.

A pond on the patio

Even a patio can provide enough space for a water garden. Waterlilies can bloom in your mini-pond, and there may even be enough room for fish. The planting containers can be wooden tubs — perhaps wine or beer barrels cut in half. They must of course be made watertight. Sometimes it's enough to leave a barrel standing in the rain for a while; the wood swells up, making the barrel watertight. A more reliable method is to line the tub with thin polythene sheeting or a pond-lining material. Fix the lining just above your intended water level, and fast-growing plants will quickly conceal it.

The advantages of wooden containers

Wooden containers are particularly suitable. Besides looking decorative and rustic, they can survive being left outside in the winter — although it helps if you put them next to a south-facing wall, or in some other warm spot that's sheltered from the wind. There are two good reasons for doing this. First, it's a terrible chore bringing them indoors to overwinter; and second, waterlilies can't stand

Old (and new) barrels make mini-garden ponds for a balcony or patio.

Dwarf waterlilies are ideal for patio ponds.

being transplanted every year. They need to go through their dormant winter state with the tub still full of water. To make absolutely certain, pile a thick protective layer of bark mulch, or a mixture of autumn leaves, as high as possible around the tub, then cover it all with polythene sheeting weighted down with stones. Another reason for choosing wooden rather than plastic containers is that in summer the water inside doesn't warm up as fast or as much in the sun. This is important, because all waterlilies need sunshine.

It's better not to keep fish in a waterlily pond. If you enjoy keeping various types of goldfish, you would be better advised to use another container. This time put in marginal and water plants, which don't need as much sun. Besides, waterlilies need an 8-in (20-cm) layer of soil at the bottom of the tub, whereas these plants can manage with 2 in (5 cm), leaving more room for the fish in the water.

Dwarf waterlilies and companions

The most suitable waterlilies for patio ponds, these don't need the water level to be more than 8–12 in (20–30 cm) deep. Good companion plants include

Scirpus tabernaemontani 'Zebrinus'; its 20-in (50-cm) long, whip-like leaf stalks have whitish, horizontal stripes. A 3-ft (1-m) diameter tub can also accommodate a water plantain (*Alisma plantago-aquatica*), which gives a surprisingly attractive display of white flower panicles from July to September. An assortment of flowering, foliage and floating plants can turn your patio pond into a much-admired feature. But remember, you can have too much of a good thing!

Planting and feeding

Planting is quite simple. Start with a layer of good, heavy garden soil about 8 in (20 cm) deep. Next put a layer of gravel about 1 in (2 cm) deep over the soil: this will keep the water clean and give the plants a firm hold. If the plants aren't growing well, they may appreciate a summer feed. But you should use special slow-release fertiliser tablets that are designed for aquatic plants; never use ordinary fertiliser.

55

Planting and aftercare

Planting containers

If you're choosing containers for balcony, patio and roof gardens you have unlimited scope for imagination and inventive flair. Balcony and window-boxes onto railings or under windows are obviously restricted to long rectangular

containers. Elsewhere the choice is up to you. Harder-wearing boxes made of reconstituted stone, terracotta, ceramic ware or plastic are preferable. Wooden boxes have a shorter life because they don't stand up to constant watering. If you really want to have wood, buy pressure-treated wooden boxes. Balcony planters made of cement or concrete are heavy and therefore unwieldy. Plastic containers are much easier to handle. They're light and they warm up quickly, which ensures that your plants always have those all-important 'warm

A huge range of plant containers is available from garden centres.

An old cattle-trough is a valuable ornament; unfortunately they are not cheap.

feet'. That also means of course that they'll need watering more often, so the best choice is probably reconstituted stone containers. These are completely unaffected by high moisture levels or by temperature changes ranging from heat waves to heavy frosts.

If you're buying new containers, look out for the ones that are narrower at the base than at the top. This allows you to stack them, so they're easier to carry and easier to store. Experience shows that it's better to use several shorter boxes rather than one longer

For lovers of the Orient, ceramic pots from China or Thailand are available in many shapes and colours.

one. It isn't just older gardeners who find it difficult to move containers about once they've been filled. Weight is an important factor, especially when you have to lift the boxes up and down between the ledge and the floor in spring, or before the first cold snaps in autumn.

When you're choosing containers for planting, always make sure they have drainage holes like those of plant pots. If they don't, the soil can easily become sour; then the roots of your plants will become diseased, their leaves will turn yellow and growth will be retarded. Of course, the holes won't be any use if the containers stand directly on a flat surface. You'll need to raise them a little, either with built-in stands that come with special terracotta feet, or else with

small wooden blocks placed underneath them.

Many people never stop to think that most patio plants grow quickly and consume large amounts of nutrients, yet they have to manage for several months in a small container. That's why your boxes should have as much space for the roots as possible: they should be at least 8-10 in (20-25 cm) high. This also means less trouble with watering, because the soil dries out less quickly than in smaller containers. If, however, you only have small containers at your disposal, then you'll have to restrict the number of plants in them accordingly. Often the plants in patio containers are much too close together, and constant watering and feeding will not overcome the problem.

If you have enough room on your patio for plant tubs and trough gardens, you can count yourself lucky. 'Tubs' and 'troughs' don't sound very exciting, but there's more to choose from than the bowls and tubs you can buy at any garden centre. Consider, for instance, really valuable items such as hand-made sandstone containers, second-hand cattle troughs, sections from old fountains, casks and wheelbarrows. Your choice is entirely a matter of taste and available space.

If you want your plantings to be more or less permanent, choose the containers with particular care. They should still appeal to you in a few years' time, and they shouldn't be so heavy that you can't easily move them at a later date. Within these limits it's always best to choose a larger container rather than a smaller one. A small one will give the plants little chance

to develop properly: they will tend to dry out, and to freeze in winter. This is a particular risk with plastic containers; it's better to use boxes and bowls made of reconstituted stone, terracotta, ceramic ware or wood.

Containers that take care of themselves

If you don't have a resident granny and you don't like bothering the neighbours, you'll have problems with watering your plant containers while you're away from home. Not many people take their holidays in winter; most go away in summer when the weather is warmest. That's also the time when containers and bowls dry out particularly quickly, and the plants they contain need a great deal of water.

Flower boxes with automatic watering systems offer an answer to this problem. There is a choice of many different systems, sizes and colours, and these containers aren't just for holiday use. They will water your plants evenly throughout the year, ensuring there is never a drought or a flood. In fact, you need never water your plants again, as long as you keep the reservoir topped up all the time.

Containers with a false base

There are several automatic watering systems on the market (e.g. Oase) that work on the following principle. A false base subdivides the container into a water reservoir and a planting space. The reservoir has a refill opening and a transparent window that allows you to keep a precise check on the water level. Wicks lead up through the false base into the soil above and supply it with the necessary moisture. It's vital to check the water level regularly.

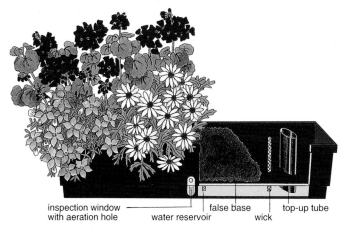

inspection window with aeration hole — water reservoir — false base — wick — top-up tube

In the Oase reservoir system, wicks supply the plants with water.

The water supply below the false base of this container will be enough for a long dry spell.

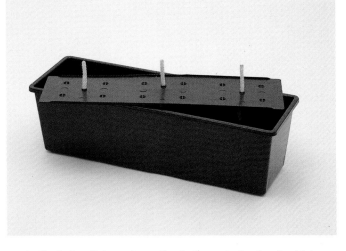

The Gardener Box

The Gardener Box is a long-term plantcare system that has proved very successful in Germany, though it is difficult to obtain in the UK. It consists of a shock-proof, fracture-resistant plant container that has double walls with a cavity in between. In a box measuring 40 × 8 × 8 in (100 × 20 × 20 cm), for example, this cavity would hold about 21 pt (12 l) of nutrient solution. The solution passes through openings in the floor between the two compartments to give the roots a regular supply, tailored to the needs of the plants. The same box would hold about 1 cu ft (20 l) of soil, which you could expect to hold about a further 7 pt (4 l) of water. The total water storage capacity would therefore be about 28 pt (16 l) — enough for a lengthy dry spell.

The box can also cope with weather at the other extreme. In a period of constant rain, for instance, surplus water can gradually drain off through small tubes in the base. A further advantage is that several boxes standing next to each other can all be supplied from a central filling point, because each can be linked to the next by sections of hose. This is even more convenient if you fit the automatic watering system, a modified box with an integral ball-valve which you simply connect to a tap.

Trickle watering

The Blumat trickle system is equipped with ceramic sensors that react to the suction of the plant roots. The greater the suction of the roots as they dry the soil, the greater the absorption potential in the soil. The ceramic sensor transmits this potential to a flexible diaphragm in the watering head, which opens the valve to the trickle pipe. When the soil is moist enough, the valve closes automatically until the roots dry out the soil again.

Depending on the size of the planting container, one or more watering units may be necessary. They can be linked together with narrow supply hoses.

This is also a perfect way to water several plants standing next to each other. It means that no problems arise when plants with different water requirements are put together in the same box. All the trickle feeders in the system react completely independently. And it's worth noting that this slow, controlled trickle system allows the plants to benefit from slightly warmed water. The trickle system is fed either directly from the mains or from a tank installed at a higher level.

It's best to fit a pressure reducer between the system and the mains. This is supplied as part of the package, and decreases the water pressure to about 15 psi (1 bar), which for safety reasons is the maximum permissible. This means it's possible to supply balcony containers at a height of up to 13 ft (4 m). If your only option is to supply the water from a storage tank, this must stand at least 20 in (0.5 m) higher than the balcony boxes for a hose length of 16 ft (5 m). It would need to be 40 in (1 m) higher than the boxes for a 32-ft (10-m) hose, and so on. Of course, the tank can be installed higher up (e.g. in the roof-space or the attic). A balcony container 40 in (100 cm) long and 8 in (20 cm) wide will need four

Blumat units, and a tub 15–20 in (40–50 cm) in diameter will need three.

Hydroponics for patio plants

Hydroponics provide a perfect method of long-term watering not just for pot plants, but for window-boxes and containers as well. All hydroponic systems work on the same simple principle. The plant in the container is set in clean, neutral expanded-clay granules, which simply provide it with support. There are no problems with watering. The plants look after themselves, and take up as much water as they currently need — over a period of two to four weeks! A water-level indicator shows exactly how much water you need to add.

The nutrient supply is foolproof, too. Special ion-exchange fertilisers, in liquid or solid form, provide a complete store of nutrients, which are released as the plants need them. You can use a closed tank, a balcony box or a tub with an overflow as a water reservoir. To prepare it, close any holes in the base with corks or resin filler, and drill a hole in one side. This should be about a fifth of the way up from the bottom: if, for example, the container is 8 in (20 cm) high overall, the hole will be about 1.5 in (4 cm) up. Now spread a thick layer of expanded-clay pellets over the bottom, stand the plants with their root balls on top of this, and continue to add clay pellets until there's just enough space left at the rim for watering. Pour in water until it runs out of the overflow. The next day, top up the water and then check the level indicator.

A simple principle — the Blumat trickle system.

Watch out for the signs of overwatering: leaves wilt, and the whole plant starts to die off (rot). Always keep a careful eye on the moisture content of the soil — or else use an automatic watering system to avoid the problem.

inclined railings. Some balcony box holders can be adjusted to any height and width with, so are suitable for all types and sizes of box. You could even convert them into H-shaped brackets for fixing a box on top of a wall or window-sill.

If you are putting up window boxes on the higher floors of a building, you can avoid trouble by placing the containers on an undertray or a shallow trough

made of zinc or plastic. This should prevent passers-by having any unfortunate experiences when you water the plants. Alternatively you can simply buy a complete window-box set, comprising plant container and undertray.

You can use the same plants in window boxes as you would in balcony boxes, planting and caring for them in exactly the same way.

Before moving the plants out onto your patio, keep them in a cool, shady place for a week or so to adjust to their new conditions.

Window-box safety

Window boxes are exactly the same as the flower boxes that are used on a balcony or patio. So they can also be mounted on a balcony rail or wall, attached to a flat wall, or placed free-standing on the patio itself.

The type of box that fits under a window will need support. Gardening retailers have various brackets for balcony boxes in a selection of materials. Some have anti-tip devices, extended supports and an adjuster for holding the sides square against

Window-box brackets with an anti-tip device are much safer.

Position: sunny, half-shaded or shaded

Some plants love a place in the sun, including the many upright and hanging varieties of geranium, *Ageratum* and lobelias, the *semperflorens* begonias, yellow slipper flowers, petunias and marigolds. However, not all of them require a south-facing position, and they can manage with a few hours of sunshine each day. In short, they can cope with a half-shaded position.

For many patio plants sun or shade is not the relevant issue; instead, think of sun and shade. The sun moves round, the foliage of nearby trees diffuses its light, and most plants are actually able to cope with a variety of positions. Fuchsia, for example, thrives in light shade, but comes to no harm in half-shaded spots with a few hours of morning or afternoon sun. It's the same with bedding or tuberous begonias and busy lizzie, which need some shade, while geraniums, petunias, slipper flowers, lobelias and heliotropes are sun-hungry but will also tolerate half-shade.

However, most plants have *some* preferences when it comes to position. Geraniums, for example, don't really like shade but are happy with a little, just like petunias and slipper flowers.

Sun worshippers: yellow slipper flowers, heliotrope and lobelia (also suitable for half-shade).

A show of flowers in the shade

In the shade (or rather in positions facing away from the sun) fuchsias show how beautifully they can bloom without sunshine. You should keep a shady corner on your balcony or patio just for fuchsias, so that everyone can appreciate these charming little shrubs. Busy lizzies will also flower in an impressive new range of colours all summer long. They go well with the large-flowered, tuberous begonias and their dense heads of blooms, and also with the sophisticated Elatior begonias, another beautiful plant from the same family.

Some plants are sensitive to wind, which can scotch their flowers and leaves (see list).

62

Bear this in mind, and where necessary use alternatives which are not affected by wind, such as the floss flower (*Ageratum*), creeping zinnia (*Sanvitalia*) and others. The wind simply passes over them, which means they're also suitable for draughty corners.

Patio plants that like and can tolerate sunshine

Floss flower, *Ageratum*
Love-lies-bleeding, *Amaranthus caudatus*
Gold coin plant, *Asteriscus*
Fibrous-rooted begonia, *Begonia semperflorens*
Elatior begonia, *Begonia × hyemalis* Elatior hybrids
Swan river daisy, *Brachycome multifida*
Browallia, *Browallia*
Slipper flower, *Calceolaria integrifolia*
Italian bellflower, *Campanula isophylla*
Prince of Wales' feathers, *Celosia argentea*
Mini-marguerite, *Chrysanthemum multicaule*
White mini-marguerite, *Chrysanthemum paludosum*
Centradenia, *Centradenia*
Cup-and-saucer plant, *Cobaea scandens*
Coleus, *Coleus* hybrids
Morning glory, *Convolvulus tricolor*
Ornamental gourd, *Cucurbita*
Dahlia, *Dahlia* hybrids
Annual dianthus, Chinese pink, *Dianthus chinensis*
Star of the Veldt, *Dimorphotheca*
Chilean glory flower, *Eccremocarpus*
Midsummer daisy, *Erigeron karvinskianus*
Blue Mauritius, *Evolvulus convolvuloides*
Cape aster, *Felicia amelloides*
Treasure flower, *Gazania* hybrids

Heliotrope, *Heliotropium*
Hop, *Humulus scandens*
Lantana, shrub verbena, *Lantana camara* hybrids
Sweet pea, *Lathyrus*
Marguerite, *Leucanthemum maximum*
Lobelia, *Lobelia erinus*
Annual alyssum, *Lobularia maritima*
Creeping snapdragon, *Maurandia barclaiana*
Melampodium, *Melampodium paludosum*
Quamoclit, *Mina lobata*
Tobacco plant, *Nicotiana*
Geranium, *Pelargonium*
Petunia, *Petunia* hybrids
Scarlet runner, *Phaseolus coccineus*
Swedish ivy, *Plectranthus coleoides*
Annual phlox, *Phlox drummondii*
Purple bell vine, *Rhodochiton atrosanguineum*
Salvia, *Salvia splendens*
Creeping zinnia, *Sanvitalia procumbens*
Scaevola, *Scaevola aemula*
Butterfly flower, *Schizanthus wisetonensis* hybrids
Cineraria, *Senecio bicolor*
Winter cherry, *Solanum muricatum*
Marigold, *Tagetes*
Golden camomile, *Tanacetum parthenium*
Black-eyed Susan, *Thunbergia alata*
Thymophyllum, *Thymophylla tenuiloba*
Nasturtium, *Tropaeolum*
Verbena, *Verbena* hybrids
Zinnia, *Zinnia*

Patio plants that tolerate sunshine and grow well in half-shade

Fibrous-rooted begonia, *Begonia semperflorens*
Elatior begonia, *Begonia ×* *hyemalis* Elatior hybrids
Tuberous begonia
White mini-marguerite, *Chrysanthemum paludosum*
Cup-and-saucer plant, *Cobaea scandens*
Ornamental gourd, *Cucurbita*
Dahlia, *Dahlia* hybrids
Blue Mauritius, *Evolvulus Convolvuloides*
Fuchsia, *Fuchsia* hybrids
Ornamental hop, *Humulus japonicus*
Busy lizzie, *Impatiens*
New Guinea impatiens, *Impatiens* hybrids
Marguerite, *Leucanthemum*
Lobelia, *Lobelia erinus*
Annual alyssum, *Lobularia maritima*
Geranium, *Pelargonium*
Petunia, *Petunia* hybrids
Swedish ivy, *Plectranthus*
Salvia, *Salvia splendens*
Winter cherry, S*olanum muricatum*
Golden camomile, *Tanacetum parthenium*
Nasturtium, *Tropaeolum*

Patio plants that tolerate shade (or half-shade with morning and evening sun)

Elatior begonia, *Begonia ×* *hyemalis* Elatior hybrids
Tuberous begonia
Busy lizzie, *Impatiens*
New Guinea impatiens, *Impatiens* New Guinea hybrids
Fuchsia, *Fuchsia* hybrids

For half-shade: lobelias, busy lizzies and tuberous begonias.

Patio plants needing shelter from the wind

Catstail, *Acalypha pendula*
Love-lies-bleeding, *Amaranthus caudatus*
Swan river daisy, *Brachycome multifida*
Browallia, *Browallia*
Bellflower, *Campanula carpatica*
Cup-and-saucer plant, *Cobaea scandens*
Chilean glory flower, *Eccremocarpus scaber*
Creeping snapdragon, *Maurandia barclaiana*
Tobacco plant, *Nicotiana* × *sanderae*
Purple bell vine, *Rhodochiton atrosanguineum*
Salvia, *Salvia splendens*
Butterfly flower, *Schizanthus* × *wisetonensis* hybrids

Patio plants that can tolerate wind

Floss flower, *Ageratum*
Fibrous-rooted begonia, *Begonia semperflorens*
Mini-marguerites, *Chrysanthemum multicaule* and *C. paludosum*
Treasure flower, *Gazania* hybrids
Busy lizzie, *Impatiens*
Marguerite, *Leucanthemum maximum*
Creeping zinnia, *Sanvitalia*
Verbena, *Verbena*

Campanulas need to be in a sheltered spot.

How to plant

In general, frost does not affect flower bulbs, early spring flowers (e.g. daisies, forget-me-nots and primroses), water plants and ornamental shrubs — not unless there just happens to be an excessively cold spell. However, tender or half-tender patio plants (e.g. geraniums and fuchsias, the summer annuals and the tub plants) are not planted out or brought outdoors from overwintering until the weather begins to warm up. To be safe from frost this is usually early June, but it can be up to two weeks later in the north.

The first essential for planting is to spread a layer of potsherds, medium gravel or expanded clay granules (of the coarsest size used in hydroponics) at the bottom of the container. It should be about 1 inch (2.5 cm) deep, and it's there to ensure that excess water can flow out freely. Without this drainage layer, the holes in the base of a container can soon become blocked.

For annuals and other short-term plants it's a good idea to use fresh soil or potting compost each year. The old soil will have been exhausted by the plants and constant watering, and even regular feeding will not give the same results. Ready-made composts have nutrients added in the right balance to give your growing plants the ideal start. Extra feeding need not begin for another four to six weeks. If you can buy prepared

loam locally, you can make your own mix, using lime-free sharp sand to improve its drainage, and composted bark or peat to make up as much as one-third of the total volume. As an alternative to sand you can use perlite. This loosens the soil and is not harmful.

If you're using home-made plant compost, you should add extra nutrients before planting up (e.g. maybe an organic-mineral compound fertiliser or a John Innes base) — but only use it at the recommended rate. The soil should be neither too dry nor too wet, and shouldn't come right to the top of your

container. Leave a space of about 1 in (2–3 cm) at the rim to ensure there's no overflow when the plants are watered. Check where the soil level is on each plant, and plant it about 5–10 mm deeper when you put it into the container. Always remember to soak the plants thoroughly in their pots beforehand: this ensures that the root ball remains undamaged. One of the most important basic rules is not to plant too close together. A patio or window-box should look like a newly laid-out flower bed. It isn't supposed to be crowded with flowers straight away, and will look much better

if it fills and flowers gradually over a longer period.

You can't get precise information about planting distances, because plant growth depends on a number of different factors. For geraniums and petunias in a single row, the planting distance should be about 8 in (20 cm) from plant to plant. For marigolds, creeping zinnias (*Sanvitalia*) or annual alyssum it should be about 4 in (10 cm).

Below *Leave a margin for watering when the containers are filled with soil.*
Right *Gently tease out dense root balls.*

Plants growing too close together can easily become exhausted, even if fed generously. Trailing plants such as hanging geraniums, petunias and Tyrolean hanging carnations are planted at an angle to encourage their natural habit.

It's advisable to plant on a dull day or towards the evening. If there's a long spell of fine weather, begin by putting the newly-planted containers in the shade, and move them to their final position later.

Finally, water the plants in thoroughly, and mist them lightly. In a very sunny position it can be a good idea to cover them with newspaper to prevent too much evaporation. Woven garden fleece is also suitable.

If you want to plant in May but are worried about late frosts, you could cover your plants with woven garden fleece. However, it must be moistened so that the pores close if there is a frost. Fleece can also protect March-planted primroses from frost damage in the same way. This delicate filmy material can be used for several years.

Watering the right way

As with houseplants, there are no hard-and-fast rules for watering plants in window-boxes and other containers. You need to think about the different requirements of the flowers, the position of the balcony or patio — and of course the weather conditions. Don't think in terms of watering two or three times a week; water regularly, and make sure the plants always have enough moisture. Plants in containers, whether large or small, are in greater danger of drying out than any others. It may be, for example, that they need watering twice a day during a hot spell in summer. On the other hand, when it's persistently dull or rainy you may not use your watering-can for days on end.

Overwatering is a particular problem with geraniums, and should be avoided just as much as excessive dryness. Even so, occasional wilting does no harm. One danger sign is when leaves become 'scorched', as gardeners call it (i.e. turn brown and become brittle). Don't just give your plants a few drops of water: soak them thoroughly, especially if the soil is a little dry. Try not to splash water on the flowers, as this can cause spots. Plants without flowers should be watered and misted only in the evening, if possible. This gives the soil, and subsequently the plants, a chance to absorb all the water they need. If you water in the morning, or even during the day, a large amount of moisture is lost by evaporation. You save water, and time, by watering in the evening.

The spring flowerers (such as forget-me-nots and primroses) should preferably be watered in

 If you install window-boxes on the higher floors of a building, it's best to stand the containers on trays or troughs made of zinc or plastic. Particularly on hot days after generous watering, water can sometimes run out of the bottom of the boxes and drip down onto the heads of people living lower down, or unsuspecting passers-by.

the morning; in autumn the same goes for ericas and chrysanthemums. This does more good to their roots, which otherwise have to spend the night feeling wet and chilly.

Regular watering is a must.

Feeding

Most ready-mixed composts contain enough nutrients for the first four to six weeks after planting. So if you plant out around the end of May, you won't need to give them their first feed until at least the end of June. You can only ensure a regular supply of nutrients by using fresh compost. If you mix your own soil (see page 66), you should add nutrients in the form of an organic–mineral compound fertiliser or John Innes base at the recommended rate. If you're using this kind of home-made compost mixture, you can wait to begin actual feeding (preferably with liquid plant food) for eight to ten weeks after planting.

Always use a liquid feed, because in this form your plants absorb the nutrients immediately. Some liquid feeds come ready to use, some have to be diluted first, and some come in solid form and have to be dissolved in water. Yellowing of the lower leaves suggests nutrient deficiency. Sometimes (e.g. in the case of geraniums) the leaf margins turn red or the lower leaves go yellow while the upper parts of the plant continue to grow. These are all sure signs of a lack of nutrients. Always use the recommended dose — higher concentrations can damage the plant. To prevent all possible risk, feed your plants in the evening or on a dull day — not in the middle of the day or in bright sunshine.

Keep the soil evenly moist between feeds. This ensures that the plants take up all the nutrients. Feeding intervals depend on the individual development of the plants. One- or two-week intervals are the usual rule, based on the intuition, observations and general experience of patio gardeners. Give short-term spring plants one or two feeds when they are established and to keep them flowering. Annual and perennial flowers, including fuchsias and geraniums, should be fed throughout the summer until later August or early September. If you have dwarf shrubs in containers, stop feeding them in August. Ericas, chrysanthemums and other autumn flowerers can manage without extra feeding.

Without feeding this magnificent display of blooms would not be possible.

The last fertiliser feeds should be given in early September. Later feeding encourages new, vigorous growth into the autumn, and stops the plants becoming hardy for the winter. Window-box or tub plants in this soft condition will not then survive in their winter quarters.

Overwintering

If you are overwintering patio plants, the only way to get satisfactory growth the following year is to keep them in a place where all their requirements are met, and to cut them back correctly if they need it.

A basement or garage should be as light as possible, and the thermometer should never go above 45°F (8°C); the ideal temperature is between 41°F and 43°F (5-6°C). Equally, the temperature should never drop below freezing. The humidity in these places is normally fairly high, so you will only occasion-

ally need to moisten the plants (you should never actually soak them). Geraniums will need a regular 'tidy' — just remove the dead and wilted leaves.

If the room chosen should get too warm, it can help to keep the window open and check the plants for water every fourteen days. It's also very important to put the plants where they can get some light. Geraniums and fuchsias are best left to over-winter in their containers. At about the end of February or the beginning of March take them out (without damaging the root balls) and replant them in fresh soil. Then stand the boxes in

A greenhouse or conservatory is the ideal place for overwintering.

the brightest spot you can find. It should also be rather warmer (up to 60°F/15°C). Give them more water: the precise amount will depend on the development of their shoots (now steadily increasing) and on the ambient temperature.

Winter quarters for plants in tubs

Almost all tub plants do best in cellars, basements, storerooms or utility rooms which have little or no heating, and are as light as possible. If the temperatures and light levels are right, these plants can also be kept successfully in garages. Again, it's best to water sparingly: the blue African lily, the agaves and the opuntias need no water for almost the entire winter. Plants which overwinter with a lot of foliage (e.g. oleanders, cordylines, date palms and other evergreens) need to be watered more than the deciduous tub plants, the bougainvilleas and the lilies that lose their foliage.

Some keen gardeners put their tub plants in a light entrance hall or on a staircase close to the window. In fact, standard marguerites can even flower here through the winter . These should not be pruned back beforehand.

A greenhouse of course can offer the ideal winter quarters for your plants. However, it will have to be heated to keep out the frost, and this is an extra expense compared to over-wintering plants indoors. You could use polythene bubble sheeting to divide your greenhouse into sections each providing different conditions, but you should be careful to ventilate adequately on sunny days.

Pruning

It's best to prune geraniums, fuchsias, angel's trumpets and standard marguerites lightly before you take them in. This helps to check any further development of the plants in their winter quarters at the outset. Cut back geraniums to just four or five 'eyes' (leaf joints with thickened sections, which are easy to recognise). Prune back fuchsias and standard marguerites to half their size, and angel's trumpets (*Datura*) even more severely; they should more or less be reduced to stumps. If leafy shoot tips more than about 3 in (8 cm) long have developed by the spring, even in a cool and bright cellar, it's best to prune these back so you can achieve a nice bushy habit.

Cutting the plants back makes more space.

Plants in their winter quarters need only a little water.

71

Propagating plants

Cuttings

After a time, overwintered balcony plants such as geraniums, fuchsias, slipper flowers and lantanas become too old or unsightly. That's the time to raise fresh, young plants by propagation from cuttings. For geraniums this technique can even replace overwintering, which is sometimes rather difficult. Besides, overwintered plants tend to look rather the worse for wear, and they will flower much later than plants grown from cuttings.

To propagate geraniums or other perennials, use a sharp knife to take **shoot-tip** cuttings. A shoot-tip cutting should be about the length of your finger, with three to five pairs of leaves. Make your cut just below the last leaf (i.e. directly under a leaf node). This is where the plant stores its reserves for the formation of side shoots and leaves, and these substances also promote fast and effective root formation.

Before you insert the cuttings, remove bottom leaves and buds. If they're geraniums, you can cut the remaining leaves in half: this reduces the surface area available for evaporation. Leave geranium cuttings for an hour or more so the cut surfaces can dry, then insert them in pots or bowls. Insert other cuttings straight away. Small peat pots (jiffy-pots) are ideal for this, or you can use plastic module trays. Here the cuttings can grow undisturbed until they're repotted into larger containers.

The best mixture is a standard commercial seed compost (or a ready-mixed potting compost), but this must be mixed with an equal quantity of lime-free sand. The best time for propagation is in July or August: at this time of year the cuttings can still make good roots before winter. The ideal rooting temperature is from 65°F to 68°F (18-20°C).

Insert the cuttings in small pots, and cover the containers with woven fleece or perforated expanding polythene sheeting. Keep them fairly moist until late autumn, and then, for the winter, put them in a bright spot that isn't too warm (46-50°F/8-10°C). Ideally they shouldn't grow much during this period. In the spring, transplant them into larger pots and pinch out the main shoots: this ensures better branching.

Propagation from seed

Many annual summer flowers can be grown from seed. A few, such as annual alyssum (*Lobularia maritima*) and mignonette, can be sown in situ, but most are **planted out**. In gardening this term means that the seed is sown in pots or seed trays in a warm place (e.g. a window-sill indoors) at temperatures between 65°F and 72°F (18-22°C). If you have a heated propagator, that will obviously do just as well.

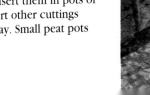

For propagating cuttings, mix sand with your compost (below).

After setting the cuttings, cover the container with polythene.

The method is fairly straight-forward. Fill your chosen container with seed compost (there are several commercial brands), and press it down lightly using a flat board. Sow the seeds thinly and evenly, and unless the seed packet gives other instructions, cover them with about 0.2 in

Any container can be used for sowing seed, but don't forget the labels!

(0.5 cm) of compost or fine lime-free sand. Finally, water them carefully using a fine rose.

Success doesn't only depend on the quality of the seed; the temperature must be right for germination, and the time must be right for sowing. You will usually find some helpful hints printed on the seed packets. I prefer to sow the seed in a small (heated) propagator, but keeping the seed container near a radiator should be enough. However, be careful not to let the soil dry out, or your efforts will come to nothing. As soon as the seeds germinate, give the tiny seedlings as much light as possible. Once they are 1.5-2 in (3-5 cm) tall, you can prick them out (transplant them into small pots), where they'll stay until they are planted in their containers.

When you're growing pansies, sow the seed from July to August at temperatures around 60-65°F (15-18°C). As it can often be hot during this period, you should keep the seed pots or trays in the shade, and cover them with newspaper, woven fleece or perforated expanding poly-thene, dampened down with water at all times. The cooling caused by evapor-ation lowers the tempera-ture. When the seeds have germinated (after about 14 days) remove the sacks, but leave the seed trays standing in the shade. To be sure that the seeds will germinate properly, rub them on the palm of your hand with some moistened, angular-grained sand. This removes an oily film surrounding the seeds that delays the germination process. Sow the seed shallowly in seed compost, keeping the compost moist at all times.

Tub plants for balcony and patio

Year after year, holidaymakers are drawn to southern Europe and the tropics by the charm of unusual plants with beautiful flowers: something that balcony and patio gardeners can enjoy every day, at least in the warmer part of the year. Besides oleander and agaves, plumbago and palms, plants for larger tubs include standard marguerites with their lovely crowns of blooms, which look like a ball-shaped flower meadow.

To these you can add annual flowers, perennials, ornamental shrubs and tougher houseplants such as hydrangeas, myrtles and Norfolk Island pines, not to mention the traditional balcony plants. Every flower that grows in a smaller container that can be moved about is just as much of a tub plant. Black-eyed Susans and cup-and-saucer plants — both superb climbers — can also be used as tub plants, just as much as bougainvilleas and climbing passion flowers.

Most tub plants like a spot in the sun, but some balconies and patios are, of course, in the shade. The sun may only come in for an hour or two each day, or perhaps not at all. In these positions fuchsias, tuberous-rooted begonias and, above all, busy lizzies, will flower well, and a number of exotic tub plants are also quite at home. The spotted laurel, for example, enjoys a position facing away from the sun. So do Chusan palms, yuccas and laurels, aralias and the scented *Pittosporum*. Even *Abutilon*, with its variegated leaves and multi-coloured flowers, will bloom here. As a rule of thumb, you could say that plants with dense foliage and large, thick leaves are more likely to tolerate shade than those with more open foliage.

With tub plants, any patio can become a flowering pot garden.

Tub plant management

Soil and repotting

Most long-lived tub plants need repotting into fresh soil every three to four years. You can mix this yourself from sand, loam and composted bark or peat, but remember to add an organic–mineral fertiliser or John Innes base. If this is too much work, you can use a ready-made loam-based potting compost such as John Innes No 3. This isn't exactly cheap, but it will be guaranteed free from diseases and weeds, as well as having extra nutrients added. Make sure the root ball stays nicely intact, and water the tub thoroughly beforehand to ensure that the roots are moist when it's placed in its new container. This in turn should be an extra 2 in (5 cm) in diameter. Don't forget to place some potsherds over the drain-age hole in order to prevent waterlogging.

Watering

Like all container plants, the tub plant's greatest enemy is dryness, because water is limited a confined container. Sun and wind also increase evaporation, so your watering can should be constantly ready for action — as often as twice a day during heat waves. Even if it's overcast or raining, the tubs still need to be watered; the leaf canopy can act like an umbrella, keeping the rain off the soil. However, be very careful not to drown oleanders and agaves, which can more easily tolerate dryness to a certain degree. Always water from above, and don't leave water standing in an undertray for hours at a time.

Standard and dwarf orange trees.

Feeding

Tub plants also depend on regular applications of fertiliser — especially those that grow quickly and have abundant

75

leaves and flowers. Fertilisers are best given in liquid form — but as always, follow all the recommendations carefully. Make sure the soil is evenly moist throughout before feeding the plant.

Pruning

Most permanent tub plants have to be cut back regularly. Among the plants that should be pruned quite hard before you

Fuchsias are the classic standards. They simply belong on a patio.

move them indoors for the winter are bush marguerites, plumbago, heliotrope, bush verbena and angel's trumpets. It's also quite in order to cut back many other plants, and this certainly helps in making room for them indoors. More mature plants respond remarkably to thinning while they are actively growing. Generally speaking, the harder you prune, the stronger the plant will grow afterwards.

Overwintering

See page 70.

Standards

With their magnificent crowns of flowers and their spheres of green leaves, standards are the aristocrats of the balcony and the tub. Fuchsias, above all, have laid the foundations of the standards' reputation. All the charm of the fuchsia flowers, which may last for months, is developed to its best advantage in the dense crowns of these balcony classics. They're available in many varieties.

Just as robust and long-flowering are the standard and bush forms of the marguerite. These produce a dense ball of meadow-like daisy flowers, either small white blooms or larger yellow ones. Shrub verbena is also obtainable in standard form, as are geraniums, hibiscus, oleander, pomegranate, plumbago, pittosporum, and myrtle. That's not all. Sweet-smelling angel's trumpets, *Anisodonta capensis*, blue-flowered species of *Solanum*, evergreen box, and bay (whose leaves can be used in the kitchen) can all be grown as standards. You can even find hydrangea and privet crowns that can be clipped to make baskets, spheres, chickens and other shapes. However this privet, unlike the hedge plant, is not frost-hardy.

In the centre, Anisodontea capensis *in bloom*

How to raise a standard-form fuchsia

First you will need a young fuchsia plant with a strong leading shoot. Remove all the flower buds, but keep the leaves and just pinch out the tips of any side shoots. This means that all the strength of the plant will go into lengthening this main shoot, which grows very rapidly as a result. To support it, and ensure that the stem grows straight, tie it to a bamboo cane. When the shoot has reached the height you want — 30 in (80 cm) for half-standards and 48 in (120 cm) for full height — pinch out the growing tip.

Now remove the side shoots lower down the stem, and leave the top ones to form the head. These must be pinched back regularly to produce a lovely symmetrical crown about 16 in (40 cm) in diameter. In nurseries this process is called 'forming' a standard. As the years go by the stem becomes thicker, and the crown grows increasingly dense.

In the late autumn you should take these standards inside to overwinter out of the frost, and cut back the fresh new growth to about 2 in (5 cm). The habit of a standard fuchsia becomes even lovelier with age, and the bell-shaped flowers increase in number from year to year. Besides fuchsias, you can produce standards from other tall-growing, bushy shrubs such as plumbago, *Cestrum*, pitto-sporum and bougainvillea. In all cases it's important to remove suckers if they appear on the stem or out of the soil.

Tub plants that are suitable for standards

Abutilon
Anisodentea
Bush marguerite, *Argyran-*
    themum frutescens
Bougainvillea
Box, *Buxus sempervirens*
Golden wonder, *Cassia*
    didymobotrya
Jessamine, *Cestrum*
Mini-orange and lemon trees,
    Citrus
Angel's trumpet, *Datura*
Cape aster, *Felicia*
Fuchsia, *Fuchsia*
Hibiscus, *Hibiscus*
Hydrangea, *Hydrangea*
Shrub verbena, *Lantana*
Bay, *Laurus*
Privet, *Ligustrum*
Myrtle, *Myrtus*
Oleander, *Nerium oleander*
Olive, *Olea*
Geranium, *Pelargonium*
Pittosporum
Leadwort, *Plumbago*
    auriculata
Pomegranate, *Punica*
    granatum
Rosemary, *Rosmarinus*
Winter cherry, *Solanum*

Tub plant profiles

name	growth habit	flowers
abutilon, *Abutilon pictum* and hybrids	shrubby, green or golden-yellow spotted leaves	bell-like, yellow and red from summer to autumn, sometimes even longer
blue African lily, *Agapanthus praecox* and other species	perennial with evergreen leaves up to 3 ft (1 m)	blue (or white) from spring to autumn
Agave, various species and varieties	leaves varying in colour, evergreen	only older plants flower here
Anisodontea capensis	shrubby, up to 3 ft (1 m) in height, particularly attractive as a standard	small, single, old-fashioned pink to dark red
bush marguerite, *Argyranthemum frutescens*	available as a bush or as a standard	white or yellow flowers, depending on variety
spotted laurel, *Aucuba japonica*	shrubby, with leathery, yellow-speckled leaves	small, insignificant, in spring
Bougainvillea glabra, B. spectabilis	rambling climber, also available as a standard (for this purpose there is a variety with white-variegated leaves)	white, pink, orange, yellow, red and (especially) crimson-purple
bottlebush, *Callistemon citrinus* and other species	shrubby, with leaves similar to myrtle, also standard forms, evergreen	brilliant red spikes from April to June, even on young plants
golden wonder, *Cassia corymbosa* and *C. didymobotrya*	free-flowering shrub with attractive, acacia-type leaves, also available as a standard	strikingly large yellow flowers in racemes from summer to autumn
orange, lemon and mini-orange, *Citrus* species and varieties	trees with shrub-like habit, evergreen	white flowers with a strong fragrance; some species will produce fruit
angel's trumpet, *Datura* (now *Brugmansia*) in several species and varieties	tall and bushy, also available as a standard	white, yellow, pink, red, single or double flowers, almost always with a strong fragrance
dragon tree, *Dracaena draco*	palm-like in habit, evergreen	large, whitish panicles, but not until the plant is old
ornamental banana, *Ensete ventricosum*	bushy, with leaves up to 10 ft (3 m) long	

requirements	propagation	overwintering/pruning
sunny position, feed and water generously, pruning stimulates growth	cuttings	light, at about 50°F (10°C), just keep the soil or compost slightly moist, cut back by half beforehand
needs full sunshine, plenty of water and fortnightly feeding until August	by division in spring	needs no light, 41-50°F (5-10°C), no pruning
needs a place in the sun, water regularly only in summer	from plantlets, offsets or seed	light, airy, at about 37-41°F (3-5°C), only water a little, can survive dry periods
bright and sunny, outdoors from June onwards, water and feed generously, but less in winter	from cuttings in spring or late summer	cool, at temperatures around 50-60°F (10-15C), prune in spring
sunny position, always remove all dead flowers, feed and water generously from March to August	cuttings	light, cool, at 41-50°F (5-10°C); water sparingly, but in a warmer hall or stairway give more water, prune hard before bringing indoors
needs half-shade (never full sun), normal amounts of water, and light feeding once or twice between June and August	cuttings at temperatures around 72°F (22°C), also possible at 54-60°F (12-15°C), but takes longer	cool, light and airy, at 41-50°F (5-10°C); don't cut back if possible, prune only young plants
sunny position, plenty of water and feeding from the end of May until August at 14-day intervals	cuttings obtained from pruning, cover and keep the pot or propagator warm (75°F/23°C)	light, airy (sunny if possible), at 41-50°F (5-10°C); keep growth under control by cutting back
sunny, airy position, keep well watered, needs feeding every 14 days (until August)	cuttings, at a soil temperature of 60-68°F (15-20°C)	light, airy, cool, at 41-50°F (5-10°C); only young plants need to be pruned back
sunny position, feed weekly from May until the end of August, water generously	from seed or cuttings (do not keep too wet)	light, airy, at 41-50°F (5-10°C); pruning necessary for young plants especially; cut back older ones only when they become too large
sunny position, water regularly, but never overwater, use a weak feed every week from April to July, repot as little as possible, use lime-free or ericaceous soil	from seed; to obtain fruit, seedlings are best grafted on to wild lemon rootstock	light, cool, at 41-50°F (5-10°C), never in a warm or dark room; shorten long shoots, otherwise prune only if necessary
sunny or half-shaded position, water and feed generously (every week from April until the end of August)	cuttings	light, cool, at 41-50°F (5-10°C); prune back hard before taking indoors, pruning also possible at any other time
sunny position, give plenty of water and feed every 14 days (from April to August)	from seed	light, cool, at 41-50°F (5-10°C), or warmer (but then give more water); no pruning
very warm, sunny position, needs generous watering and feeding	from seed, grow up to 3 ft (1 m) high in the first year	light, at temperatures of 46-55°F (8-12°C) and warmer; no pruning

Tub plant profiles

name	growth habit	flowers
edible fig, *Ficus carica*	upright, shrubby	small and insignificant
rose of China, *Hibiscus rosa-sinensis*	shrubby, very pretty as a standard	single and double flowers in various colours, some bi-coloured
shrub verbena, *Lantana camara* hybrids	upright, also trailing varieties for hanging baskets; standards also available	flowers in many beautiful, glowing pastel shades
laurel or bay, *Laurus nobilis*	upright habit, also standard, globular and pyramidal forms, one variety with white leaf tips, evergreen	yellowish, insignificant
oleander, *Nerium oleander* in many varieties	shrubby, also as a standard, evergreen	single to double flowers, large range of colours: from white to yellow, salmon, pink and red
olive, *Olea europaea*	tree-like, evergreen	blooms regularly and may produce fruit (olives)
date palm, *Phoenix canariensis*	forms a trunk, with long fronds, evergreen	flowers only appear on older plants
Pittosporum, various species	shrubby, evergreen	white flowers, turning yellow, with a magnificent fragrance
leadwort, *Plumbago auriculata*	climbing, train as a bush by pruning and tying up	blue or white flowers
pomegranate, *Punica granatum*	shrubby, deciduous; there is also a dwarf form	mostly red, but also orange, yellow and white, plus double varieties
Solanum (now *Lycianthes*) *rantonettii, S. jasminoides, S. wendlandii, S. laciniatum*	shrubby, *S. rantonettii* like a climbing shrub	pale to dark blue, also purple, from June to October (and longer)
glory bush, *Tibouchina*	shrub-like habit, evergreen, leaves covered with soft hairs	velvety bluish-purple
Chusan palm, *Trachycarpus fortunei*	forms a trunk, magnificent fronds	only older plants will flower
palm lily, *Yucca* — as tub plants: *Y. aloifolia,* and *Y. gloriosa*	forms a trunk (*Y. aloifolia*), bush-like (*Y. gloriosa*)	white, pink-tinged flowers

requirements	propagation	overwintering/pruning
full sunshine, plenty of water, feeding (fortnightly) from April to the end of August	cuttings (6-8 in/15-20 cm long), layering	light, cool, airy, at 46-55°F (8-12°C); cut back older plants to encourage fruiting
sunny, sheltered from wind and rain, water regularly, feed every 14 days from April to August when growing strongly	cuttings, also from seed	light, warm, not below 60°F (15°C) (in the house or conservatory), but water sparingly; cut back shoots by two thirds
sunny, water regularly, do not forget to feed (preferably once a week)	cuttings from August/September onwards; pinch out shoot tips several times as they grow	light at 41-50°F (5-10°C); prune shoots by about two thirds before taking in
sunny position, generous watering, feed each week from April to August	cuttings, use heated propagator or keep compost warm	light, cool, at 41-50°F (5-10°C), not too dark; cut back and shape in March/April
sunny, regular watering, feed every eight days from April to August	cuttings (soft tip cuttings will root in water)	light, cool, at 41-45°F (5-8°C); don't cut off unopened buds as these flower in the following year; only old plants should be severely pruned
sunny position, regular watering, feed only once a month from April to August	cuttings, also from seed (takes much longer)	light, cool, at 41-50°F (5-10°C), doesn't matter if leaves are shed; cut back as necessary
sunny, relatively little watering and feeding, transplant only when absolutely necessary	from seed	light, cool, at 41-50°F (5-10°C), not warmer
sunny position, water regularly and feed every 14 days from April to August	from seeds or cuttings	light, cool, at 41-50°F (5-10°C); may be cut back, but this is not essential
sunny position, water regularly and feed every 14 days from April to August	cuttings	light, cool, at 41-50°F (5-10°C); cut back shoots by half before taking in
sunny, not too much water, feed every four weeks from April until July	cuttings, also from seed	cool, light, at 37-41°F (3-5°C) (if possible not warmer); reduce shoot length by one-third before taking in
generous watering and feeding every 14 days from May to October	cuttings	prune back hard and stand in a cool, dark place
bright conditions, water and feed generously, keep almost dry after flowering	from cuttings, use heated propagator or keep soil warm	cool, at 50-55°F (10-12°C); prune back, keep virtually dry, even if a new shoot appears
sunny position, water regularly, feed every 14 days from May to June	from seed	cool, at 41-45°F (5-8°C), but also over-winters in a heated living room just as well as in a dark, front-free position
very sunny, generous watering and feeding	by division, taking off side shoots, or from seed	no difficulty in overwintering in cool or warm room

Pests and diseases

The well-being and health of your plants depends on good soil mixed with a balanced fertiliser in the right amounts, and on regular supplies of water and nutrients. You also have to take individual needs into account. If you neglect any of these factors the plants soon begin to suffer, and disease and pests move in. If the plants are weakened these will spread particularly rapidly, meeting little resistance.

There are many products that will protect your plants, including some that are environmentally friendly, or harmless to useful insects. We can certainly control plant diseases caused by fungi, and we can destroy aphids and other pests, but that begs the question. Is it worth using these products?

It's certainly worthwhile for perennials, and long-lived plants, such as fuchsias and geraniums, which are going to be overwintered. The same goes for oleander, palms, angel's trumpet and ornamental shrubs, but not for summer annuals (in most cases), as these will die anyway when the frost comes; it's therefore best to dispose of any sick plants as quickly as possible, so they don't infect their healthy neighbours. You can quickly fill up the gaps they leave, and it won't cost much, either. It's more important to ensure the best possible con-

ditions from the outset and throughout the growing season, and to give plants the best possible protection wherever you decide to overwinter them.

The commonest pests

Aphids

Sap-sucking, green, grey or black, wingless or sometimes winged insects.

Damage symptoms: Stunting, leaf curl, and similar malformations in other parts of the plant, generally retarded growth; the result of aphid infestation is black, sooty mould on the lower

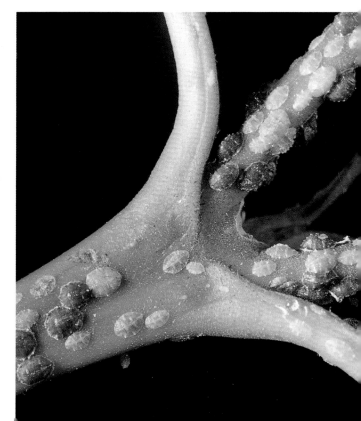

leaves, because their sticky excretions are colonised by the mould fungus.

Preventative measures: Give plants a balanced diet.

Direct action: To protect the natural predators (ladybirds, green lacewings, hoverflies etc.) spray only with plant protection products of natural origin such as derris or natural fatty acids

Right *Aphids are among the most common pests.*

Below *Irregular watering encourages infestation by scale insects.*

(soaps). Spray only where there are pests, including the leaf undersides, until the liquid just begins to run off; repeat as recommended by the manufacturer. The ICI Big Gun, which contains an extract of the pyrethrum leaf, is used in the same way, with immediate effects.

Scale insects and mealy bugs

Scale insects can be recognised from their upturned basin- or comma-shaped scale shells; mealy bugs are woolly-white, mobile insects.

Damage symptoms: Plants disfigured, parts of plants

83

Left *The 'cobwebs' indicate infestation by spider mites.*

Above *Whitefly are mostly found on the leaf undersides.*

covered in sooty mould (see aphidson page 82); the bugs settle in the leaf bases, on stems and on leaf undersides, especially on plants with hard leaves.

Preventative measures: Keep plants healthy and well fed, and water them regularly. Dryness encourages infestation by scale.

Direct action: The young (mobile) scale insects can be controlled by sprays containing permethrin, but always test-spray a small piece first, as some plants are sensitive under certain conditions. If the infestation is severe, repeat doses may be necessary. The use of pyrethrum sprays may also give some control.

Red spider mite

A minute green, yellow or reddish, oval-shaped spider mite.

Damage symptoms: Leaf undersides covered with delicate webs; leaves become discoloured with spots, turn yellow and then brown before dropping.

Preventative measures: Always give the plants enough water, especially when temperatures are high and there are long periods of sunshine. Avoid overfeeding. If possible put affected plants in the shade. Spray the undersides of leaves with cold water, and sprinkle water around containers to raise humidity.

Direct action: Control as for aphids — i.e. treat by spraying with derris or by using permethrin. Here again, repeat treatments will be almost essential, as these are difficult pests to control.

Whitefly

Very small white, moth-like insects with roof-shaped wings, which spread rapidly, often in vast numbers. The larvae and adults feed by sucking sap from the leaf undersides.

Damage symptoms: The insects are very easy to see, and cause yellow spots on leaves, which then die off; they also cover the leaves with sooty moulds. Whitefly are particularly common on fuchsias, shrub verbenas, slipper flowers, *Ageratum*, sage and tomatoes.

Preventative measures: Keep the plants healthy and well fed, but don't overfeed them with nitrogen fertiliser.

Direct action: Spray only with permethrin-based insecticides — other types are ineffective. Repeat doses will be essential in order to control successive generations. As an extra measure, it's possible to use yellow sticky cards, which work on the same principle as flypapers. Since the whitefly dies in low temperatures, it should become less of a problem once the plants are in winter quarters, or if they are outdoors in cool weather during spring or autumn.

Caterpillars

Caterpillars are occasionally found on patio or balcony plants. During the day they're generally on the undersides of the leaves or in the soil, feeding only at night.

Damage symptoms: Round holes in the leaves where the caterpillars have been feeding.

Preventative measures: Pick off the caterpillars and dispose of them. They are often butterfly caterpillars, which can be released among wild plants or weeds, and may survive there.

Direct action: use a purely biological caterpillar treatment, a powder spray of *Bacillus thuringiensis*. The powder must be dissolved in water before use.

The main fungal diseases

Powdery mildew

A floury, greyish-white coating appears on the leaves, stalks and stems. The leaves may wilt, shrivel and drop. Begonias, forget-me-nots and roses are particularly affected.

Powdery mildew appears as a greyish-white deposit. Eventually the leaves shrivel and drop.

Preventative measures: Avoid overfeeding, especially with nitrogen-rich fertilisers.

Direct action: Cut off the affected parts of the plants, or collect them up and throw them into the compost bin. Destroy badly affected plants completely. At the first signs of infestation, spray the affected plants with a mildew spray such as Nimrod T which doesn't harm useful insects. Preventative use of fungicides spray is always advisable, especially for begonias.

In the case of viral diseases — this is mosaic disease — the affected parts of the plant should be removed immediately.

Direct action: Cut off affected parts (always wash the knife afterwards), and throw them into the dustbin. Put the affected plants in a light, dry, well-ventilated place, and don't feed them again until they have recovered.

Leaf spot disease

Various fungi cause rounded or angular, often merging spots on the leaves, which enlarge rapidly. The leaf margins will often turn brown. This usually occurs during wet weather.

Preventative measures: Water and feed regularly. Always take account of specific plant requirements.

Direct action: Remove and dispose of the affected parts of the plants.

Grey mould (Botrytis)

Easily recognisable by the dense, grey cushions of mould, which give off dust. Can appear on all parts of the plant, and especially on plants growing or overwintering in cool, humid conditions. Geraniums, fuchsias and begonias are most at risk.

Preventative measures: Don't plant too close. Remove damaged foliage. Ensure a balanced diet that isn't too rich in nitrogen. Water only in the mornings or afternoons, so that the plants are dry again by evening. Avoid overwatering.

Rust

The leaves become speckled with orange, rust-red or brown pustules, then turn yellow and drop. On geraniums there are very noticeable red pustules arranged in rings on the under-sides of the leaves. The plants most at risk are geraniums, carnations and roses.

Direct action: Remove and dispose of the affected parts of the plant. Rust is difficult to control. Use Synthane if the problem persists.

Viral diseases

Viral diseases interrupt the growth of the plant. They are not always recognised at once because they only rarely cause the plant to die.

Mosaic disease can be recognised by irregular spots or streaks of white or yellow on leaves, or of pale or dark colour on flowers. The plants most affected are begonias, geraniums, primulas and tulips.

Leaf curl causes the leaves to curl, buckle upwards and wrinkle; the flowers are deformed.

When a plant is affected by **yellowing virus**, the leaves turn yellow or yellowish-green. Shoots or entire plants may be stunted and brown, become brittle or unexpectedly produce dwarf forms.

Cure: You cannot treat viral diseases directly with plant protection products. You can avoid them by controlling sap-sucking insects, which often carry the diseases to healthy plants from those already affected. Aphids and thrips transmit viruses. It's best to dig up and burn diseased plants. At the very least, you should cut off and dispose of all the affected areas on each plant straight away.

These pelargoniums show the tell-tale signs of blackleg disease.

87

A kitchen garden on the patio

Vegetables

If you want your vegetables to flourish, the first important thing is a container that is the right size for the crop. In order to grow to your satisfaction, many vegetables prefer soil 8-12 in (20-30 cm) deep that contains high levels of nutrients and humus. As a guide, a tomato plant needs a container that can hold 0.3 cu ft (8-10 l) of soil. You can only guarantee getting proper levels of nutrients and water to the plant if your is large enough. Containers with an automatic watering system are particularly suitable for vegetables.

It's best to provide nutrients in the form of organic or slow-release fertilisers (e.g. blood, fish and bone, or Osmocote), which are also used for flowers. With these fertilisers (and others) there's absolutely no risk of overfeeding or burning. Further weekly feeding should be in liquid form.

The number one balcony and patio vegetable is the tomato, and there are special varieties you can grow in containers. These are small-fruited (or in some cases cherry-sized) tomatoes such as 'Tiny Tim', 'Sweet 100 F1 hybrids' and 'Gardener's Delight'. There are also others with yellow or plum-type fruits of standard size such as the bush tomato 'Golden Boy', which is particularly suitable for container growing. The variety 'Tumbler' is simply *made* for the patio, but is also good in hanging baskets, where it produces an abundance of small fruits, constantly changing in colour. Tomatoes need lots of water and a weekly feed; if possible you should also find them a spot that's sheltered from the rain. As in the garden, tall-growing tomatoes on a patio or balcony should have their side shoots regularly pinched out. They can be planted out from late May onwards.

If your balcony or patio faces south you can also grow peppers and aubergines alongside your tomatoes, but they both need plenty of sun. There is also room here for trailing marrows of the long green or yellow disc-shaped type, which can to be trained up supports, or for bush types and green and yellow courgettes, which are bushy and stay on the ground.

If there are only a few hours of sun on your patio, you can grow cucumbers, radishes, peas, loosehead lettuce and all kinds of beans, as well as tomatoes,

courgettes and peppers. Climbing French and runner beans are particularly good on the balcony because they are space-saving, grow upwards and provide a dense screen and a bumper harvest. Sow in April or May.

If you like to pick fresh lettuce, go for the loosehead 'cut-and-come-again' type. This doesn't have a firm head, but it will give you a supply of tasty leaves from May to October.

Right *Cucumbers in a pot*

Below *This patio contains strawberries, tomatoes and herbs.*

Pick them at the base, leaving the roots, so that new leaves grow continuously. Sow these from March to August in a row and thin them out till they're 6–8 in (15–20 cm) apart. Varieties include 'Salad Bowl' and the red-leaved 'Lollo Rosso'.

It's fun to grow cucumbers, but for this you need a patio with only a little sun, and that's also sheltered from the wind. You'll also need climbing trellises and some large containers at least 8 in (20 cm) deep and wide. It's best to raise the cucumbers from seed indoors on a window-sill, preferably over a radiator at about 72°F (22°C); the seeds are sown in small pots in April, and planted out from late May onwards. It's

important to choose the right variety, which should be free of any bitter taste, mildew-resistant and all-female. Fruits are formed on all-female types without pollination by insects.

Varieties with all these good features are 'Bella' (with long fruits) and 'Paska' (with short fruits). It's a good idea to stand all vegetable containers in a shady place after sowing, and to cover them with woven fleece or perforated expanding polythene sheeting. This keeps the containers nice and warm, which in turn speeds up germination and removes the risk of drying out. Later on — but preferably not until after germination — you can move your pots to the desired position.

89

A varied mixture: culinary herbs, particularly parsley, along with flowering plants.

Culinary herbs

You should have at least one balcony box (or a container the same general size) for growing herbs. It's well worthwhile to be able to pick fresh culinary herbs from the balcony almost the whole year round. Besides, it doesn't take much effort to grow and look after herbs, and the plants do even better in balcony boxes and other containers than they would in a bed in the garden.

That's not all. Boxes and trays for herbs needn't be anything like as large as the ones you'd use for vegetables. They need a lot less water, and virtually no supplementary feeding — proprietary compost already contains enough nutrients for them. Only the perennials will need to be given a supply of nutrients every spring. Bear in mind that there are annual herbs (which are grown from seed each year in the spring, generally in April or May) and perennials (whose leaves die off in autumn and re-shoot in spring0. Lavender, rosemary and thyme stay green in the winter. In a balcony box 12–20 in (30–50 cm) long, one sowing of seeds for an annual should be enough — except, perhaps, in the case of dill. You may need more of this important herb, so successive sowings at three to four week intervals are advisable.

Apart from dill, other important annual herbs are borage (and one plant of this is sufficient, so pull up any others), basil, summer savory, lovage, chervil and annual marjoram, which is best raised in small pots. Growing annual herbs from seed is better than buying the small pot herbs (sold on markets and elsewhere) and planting them in your containers, which rarely succeeds as well.

Of the perennial herbs — parsley, of course — is also one of the most useful. You should always have a 12 in (30 cm) box full of this herb. Again I would recommend successive sowings at three-week intervals. Apart from the familiar curly-leaved parsley you should try the plain-leaved variety, which has a particularly aromatic flavour. Two chive plants are enough, unless you intend to force some in winter (i.e. to keep one plant in a suitably large container on the kitchen window-sill). In that case you'll need at least three plants.

For tarragon, however, one plant is enough (ask for the 'French' one, it's more aromatic). The same goes for lovage, but this needs a separate container of its own: it grows too tall and spreads too much for a balcony box. Perennial marjoram, on the other hand, is more suitable, as it remains small and dainty. I'd also recommend lemon balm, though it does tend to grow profusely. Lavender can be regarded as an ornamental plant, and is a slow-growing shrub with wonderfully fragrant leaves.

Other plants which flourish on the balcony are perennial rosemary and — for lovers of Italian cuisine — the indispensable thyme and oregano. Sage also grows well, and there are purple and golden-leaved forms. All perennial herbs need some protection in winter. Take the boxes down from the balcony ledge or window-sill, place them against the wall, and cover them with bark mulch or straw. It's important to water them regularly, even in winter, except when the soil is frozen. Rosemary is best overwintered indoors, as it may be tender in some areas. Herbs need sunshine: they'll get it on south-, east- and west-facing patios and balconies. But even on a north-facing patio or balcony you can grow chives, lemon balm, chervil or borage, and water cress, which is very high in vitamin C.

Left to right: marjoram, lemon balm, tarragon, lovage and parsley.

Fruit

If space is restricted on your balcony, it's best to trail your strawberries down from a hanging container, or train them up pyramidal supports. Use special varieties, obtainable (with the appropriate instructions) from garden stores or by mail order. I highly recommend the small-fruited perpetuals, which still retain the flavour of wild strawberries. These all fruit continuously from early summer into the late autumn. Plant them in a mixture of ready-made compost (two-thirds) and bark humus (one-third), water them generously, and give them a weak feed with liquid organic fertiliser every fourteen days from April to August.

The strawberry plants, which should not be exposed to blazing sunshine, overwinter outdoors. Simply take down the boxes or hanging baskets and stand them close to the wall. In addition, they can be protected by bark mulch. You can also expect a good harvest from red and white standard currants, though not until the second year. They're particularly good for patios because they are upright, and because their attractive, round crowns can be cut back according to the space available without any damage to the plants. For pruning, remember the basic rule: remove any shoots that cross each other and rub together.

One of the most delightful harvests, of course, will be from your mini fruit trees. Special varieties of apples, pears, cherries, peaches and nectarines, red, blue and yellow plums are obtainable, though not in every garden centre or nursery. You generally have to buy these by mail order.

The apple 'Ballerina' is particularly good: the little trees are just 12 in (30 cm) across and you need only a 24 in (60 cm) space between trees. They are columnar in habit and easy to care for. Pruning, which many gardeners find difficult, is no problem here; in fact it hardly needs doing at all. The occasional side shoot that grown too long should be cut back to three eyes.

Above *Apple trees in pots*

Left *Small-fruited perpetual strawberries*

The trees begin to bear in the second year after planting. To ensure the flowers are fertilised, it's a good idea to have at least two varieties — even if you have a so-called self-pollinating type. The mini-trees need a sunny, sheltered position. Be sure to give them plenty of water and feed them from March to August. If the roots grow out of the pots, re-pot the tree. In winter they can be kept in 'winter quarters' with other tub plants, or they can stay outside, well wrapped up. This means putting them in a box, filling the spaces with wood shavings, polystyrene chips or crumpled newspaper and sealing them in with polythene.

On a really sunny patio or balcony, you can with luck expect to produce a few sugar-sweet figs. Just a few hours of sunshine each day is all they need. They should also be given a warm, sheltered position, plenty of water in the summer, and weekly feeds from April to September. Figs are over-wintered in the same way as oleander and other tub plants. In the autumn you should give some of the older stems a hard pruning to encourage fruiting.

Wild flowers

A flower meadow on a patio or in a window-box doesn't have to be an impossible dream; it's possible to buy wild-flower seeds such as corncockle, poppies, *Phacelia*, scabious and many more. You can put together your own individual meadow-flower collection, and you might consider mixing in a few English marigolds, pheasant's eye and mignonettes, or herbs such as chervil, borage or camomile.

No need to search out wild flowers amid the wreckage of a machine-cut hedgerow — this is illegal anyway! You can find an varied assortment of flowers for the nature garden at your garden centre or gardening shop. I particularly recommend a low-growing wild-flower mixture (averaging 10–12 in/25–30 cm) that includes more than twenty different species, some of which are always in bloom. It's called 'Flowering Lawn

Mixture' from John Chambers, the wild-flower expert. All these flowers become popular landing sites for bees and butterflies looking for nectar. They also attract ladybirds, hoverflies and other useful insects. This happens in the middle of town, and of course in the country — indeed in any place where there's sunshine and shelter from wind.

Sow the seeds broadcast from April to June in a container of poor garden soil. Don't use the usual pre-packed composts unless they're mixed half and half with sand first. Better still is a mixture of sand and garden soil. The seed should be lightly scratched into the surface, no more than 0.5 in (1 cm) deep, and must be kept uniformly moist. Depending on the air and soil temperatures it may be ten or sometimes even twenty days before the seeds start to germinate. About four to six weeks later, the 'meadow' will begin to bloom. It won't stop flowering until late autumn, when the traditional balcony plants are taken in for the winter.

Wild-flower mixtures contain up to twenty different species.

A bird box is ideal for watching birds from the house.

Bird life

It isn't difficult to provide bees and butterflies with a place to live on a balcony or patio. However, if you want to give the birds a chance to nest and raise their young undisturbed, you'll need a larger space with enough room for a quiet area. And nesting boxes should only be fitted on ground- or first-floor balconies, or you'll make life very strenuous for the adult birds when they're trying to feed their young. Nesting birds need extreme quiet: if there's constant loud conversation all around the nest, the young birds will not be properly looked after.

If you want to do our feathered friends a good turn, put out earthenware or china bowls of water in summer. Thirsty birds (and insects) will be very glad to use them. Winter feeding can only really be justified if you want to watch the behaviour of wild birds in the neighbourhood. This is particularly instructive for children, and is also very enjoyable and relaxing for older people. It's important not to start feeding until the birds have no other sources of food — for example, when there's a thick covering of snow and/or continuous frost. Then you should provide several feeding places: this minimises the danger from cats, and the competition between different bird species. Proper bird-feeders guarantee hygiene and prevent infection. At all events, it's important to ensure that a bird table or other feeding area is covered by a roof to keep off the rain.

Index